Rediscovering the
Victorian Still Life

Compositions of Elegant Florals and Ornate Vintage Objects

Coloring Book

Crystal Moon

ISBN: 978-0-9888737-7-3

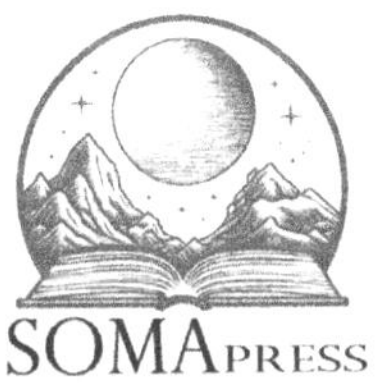

SOMA PRESS

Copyright 2023 Soma Press
All rights reserved

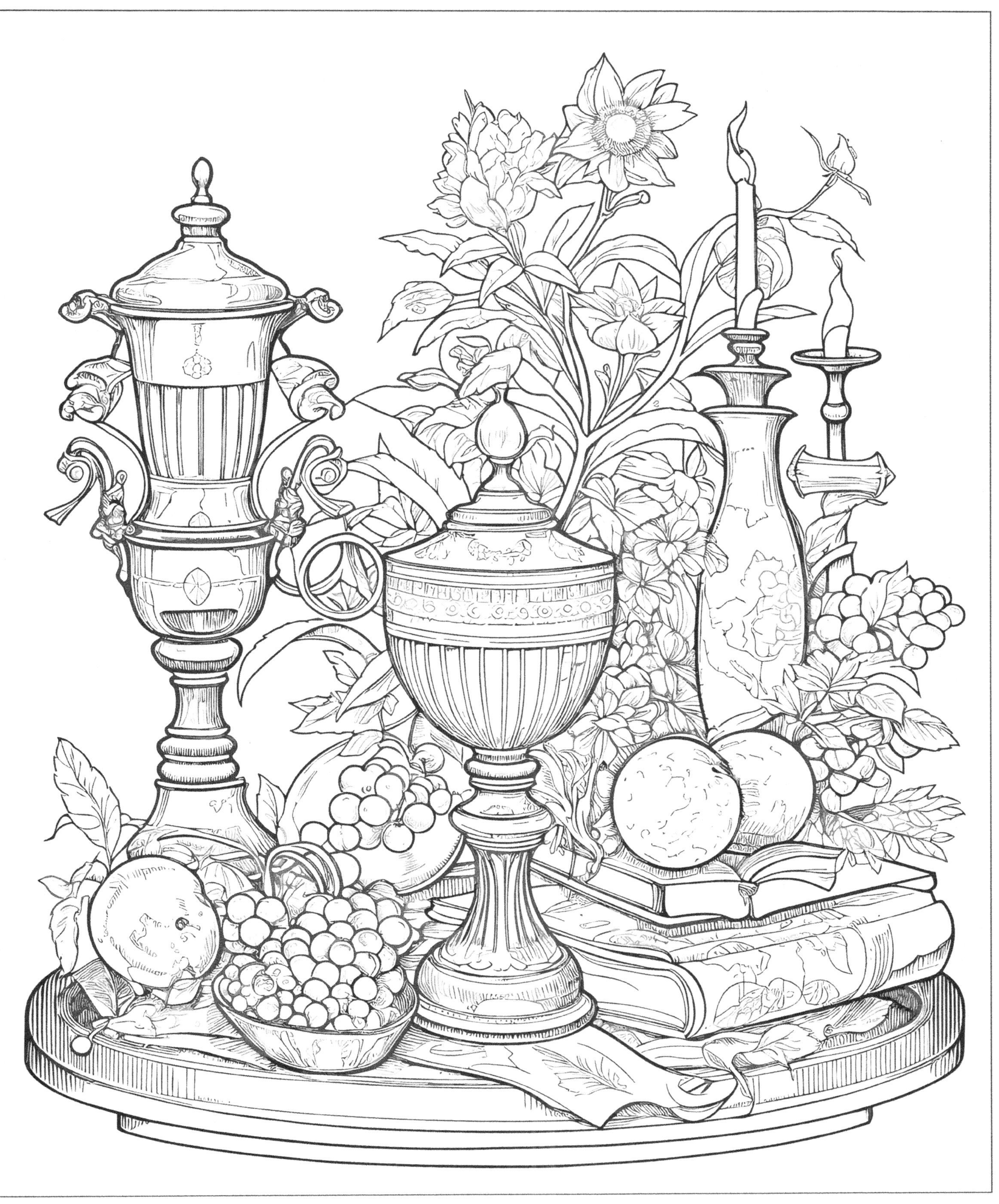

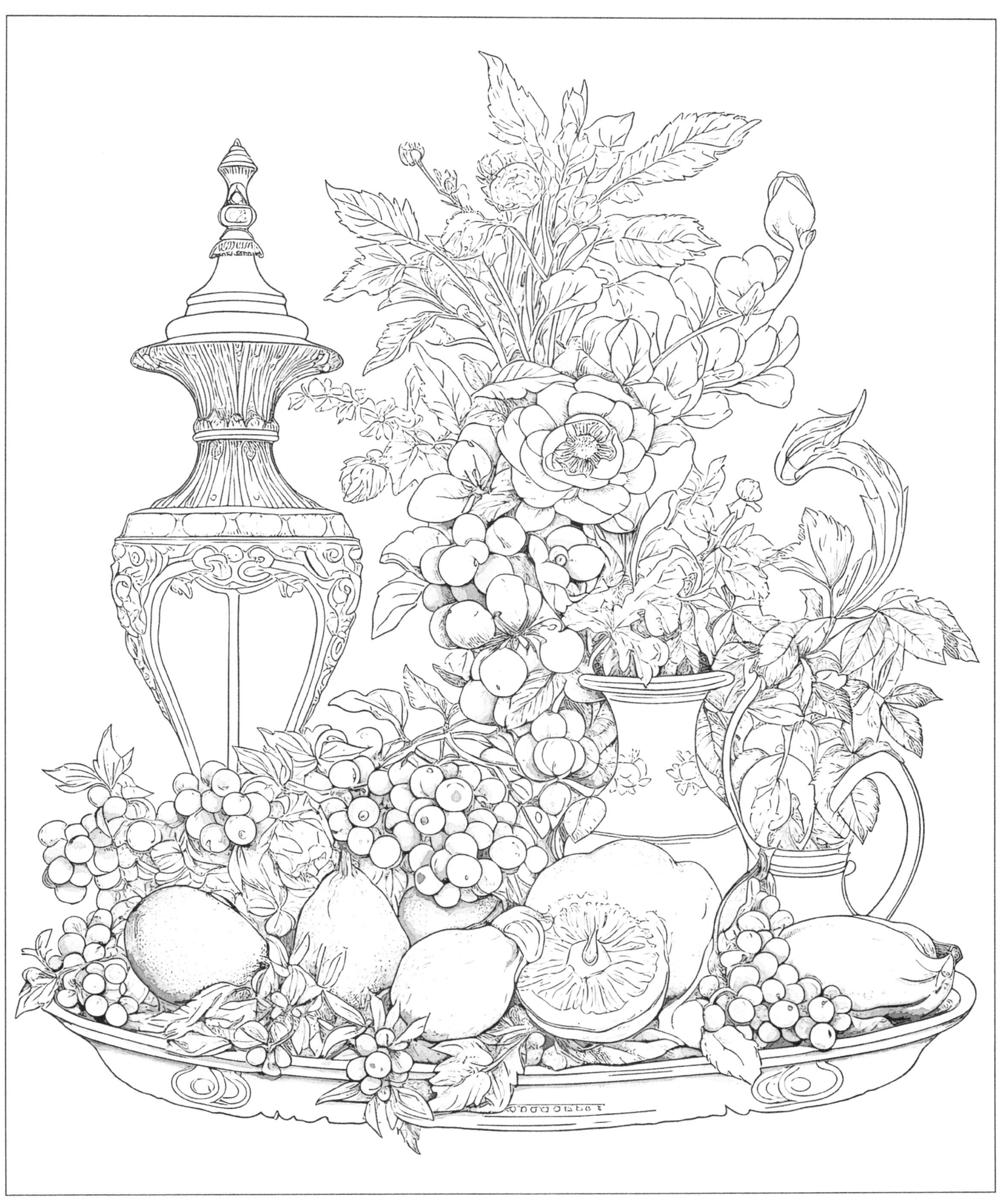

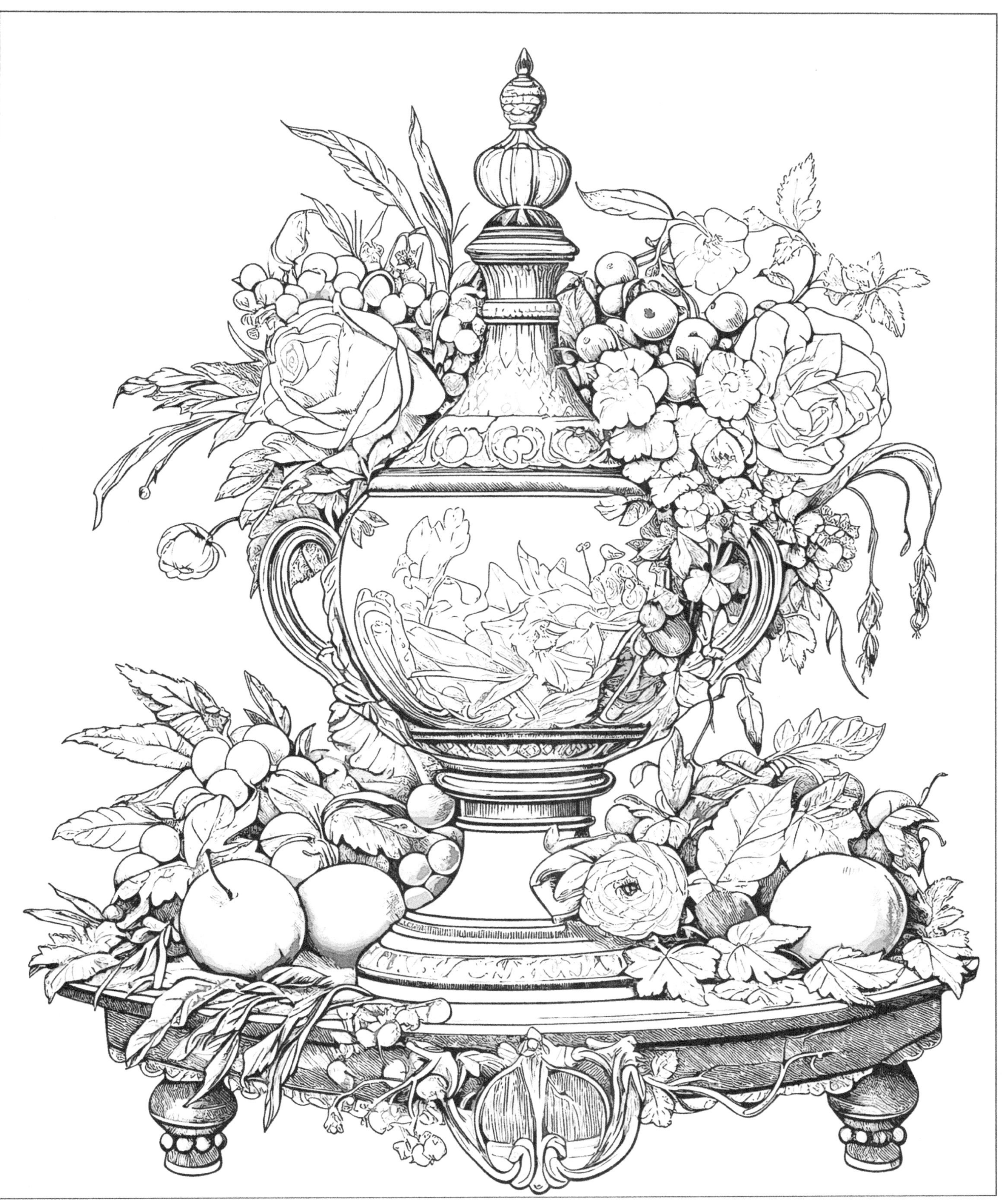

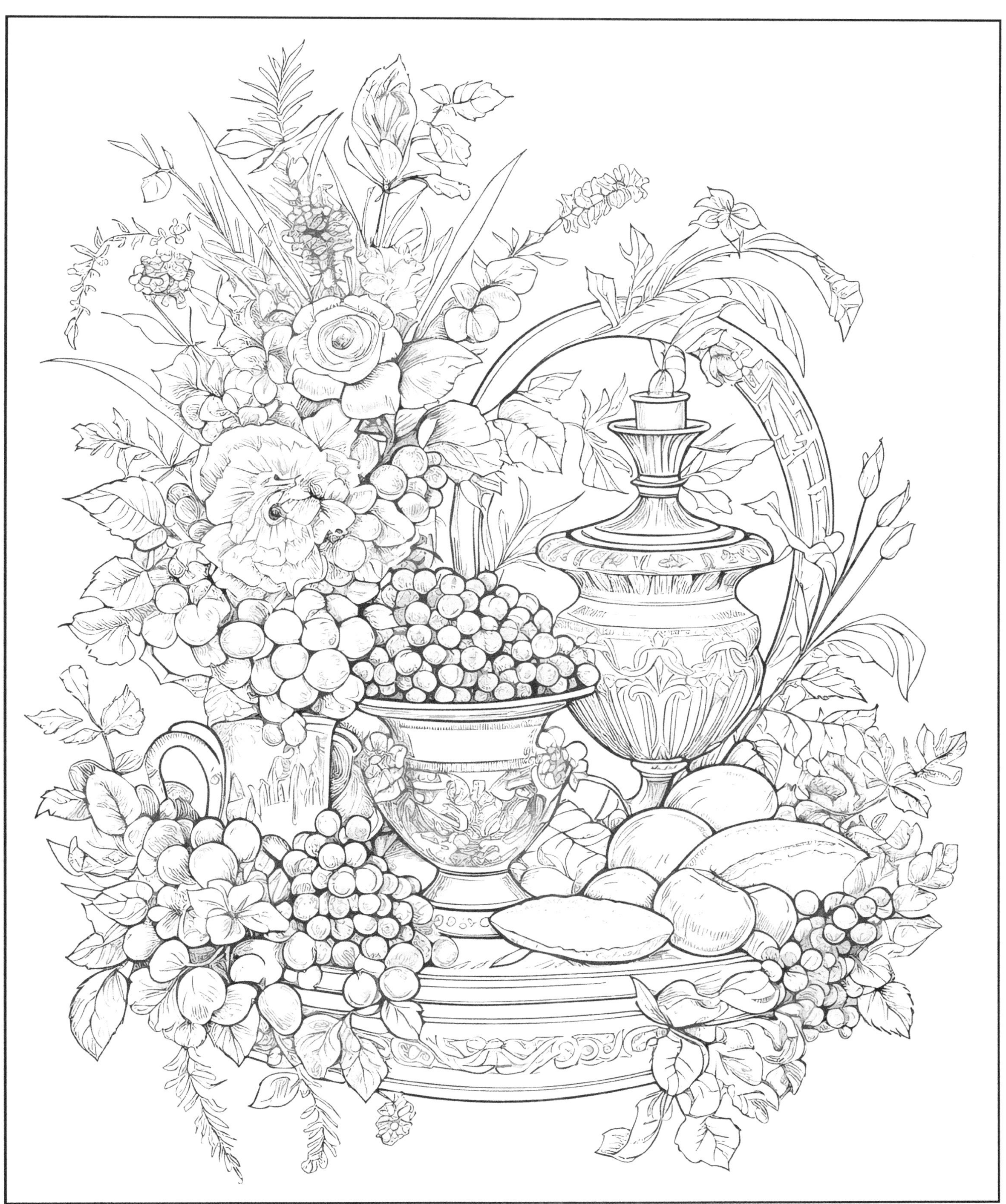

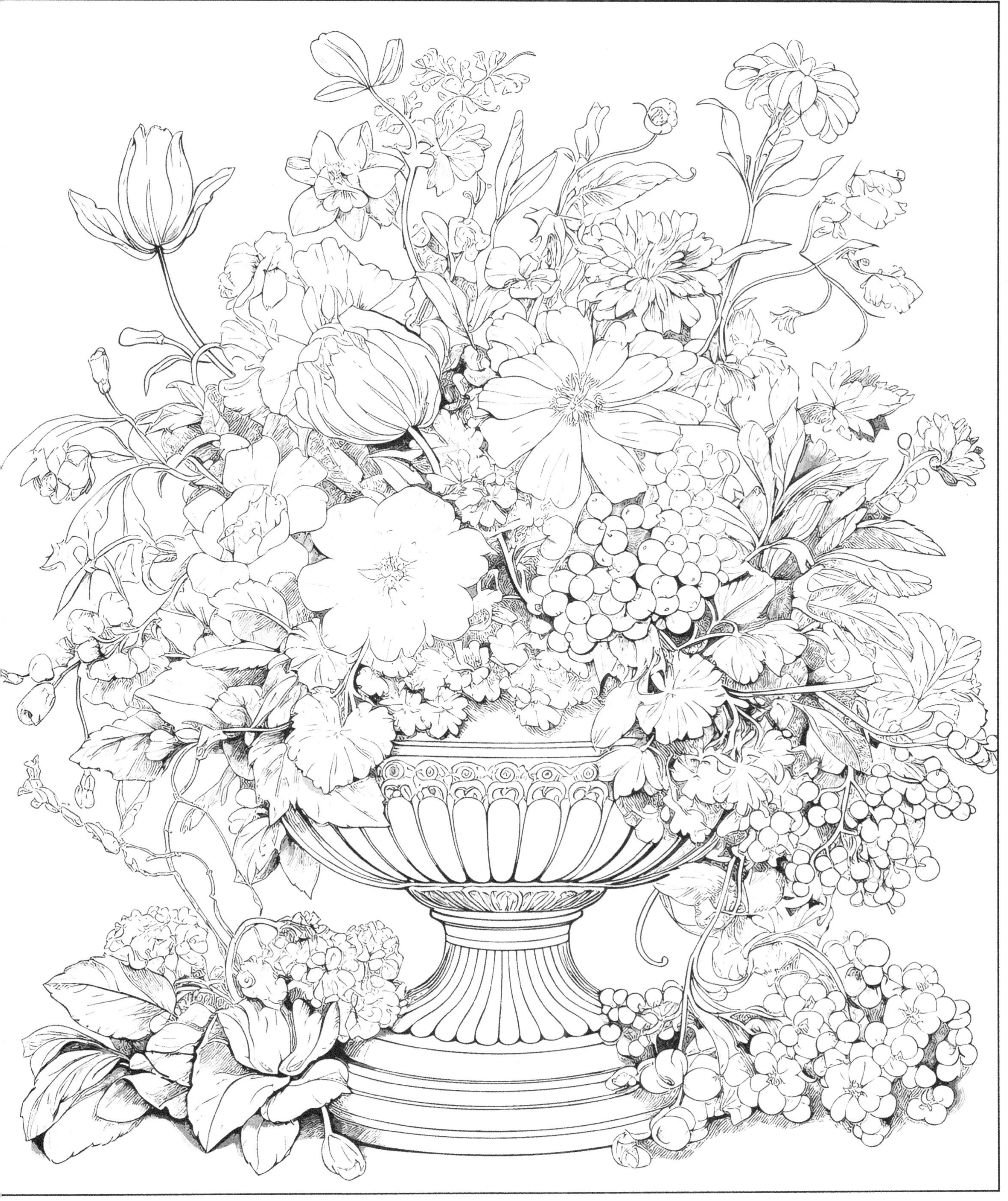

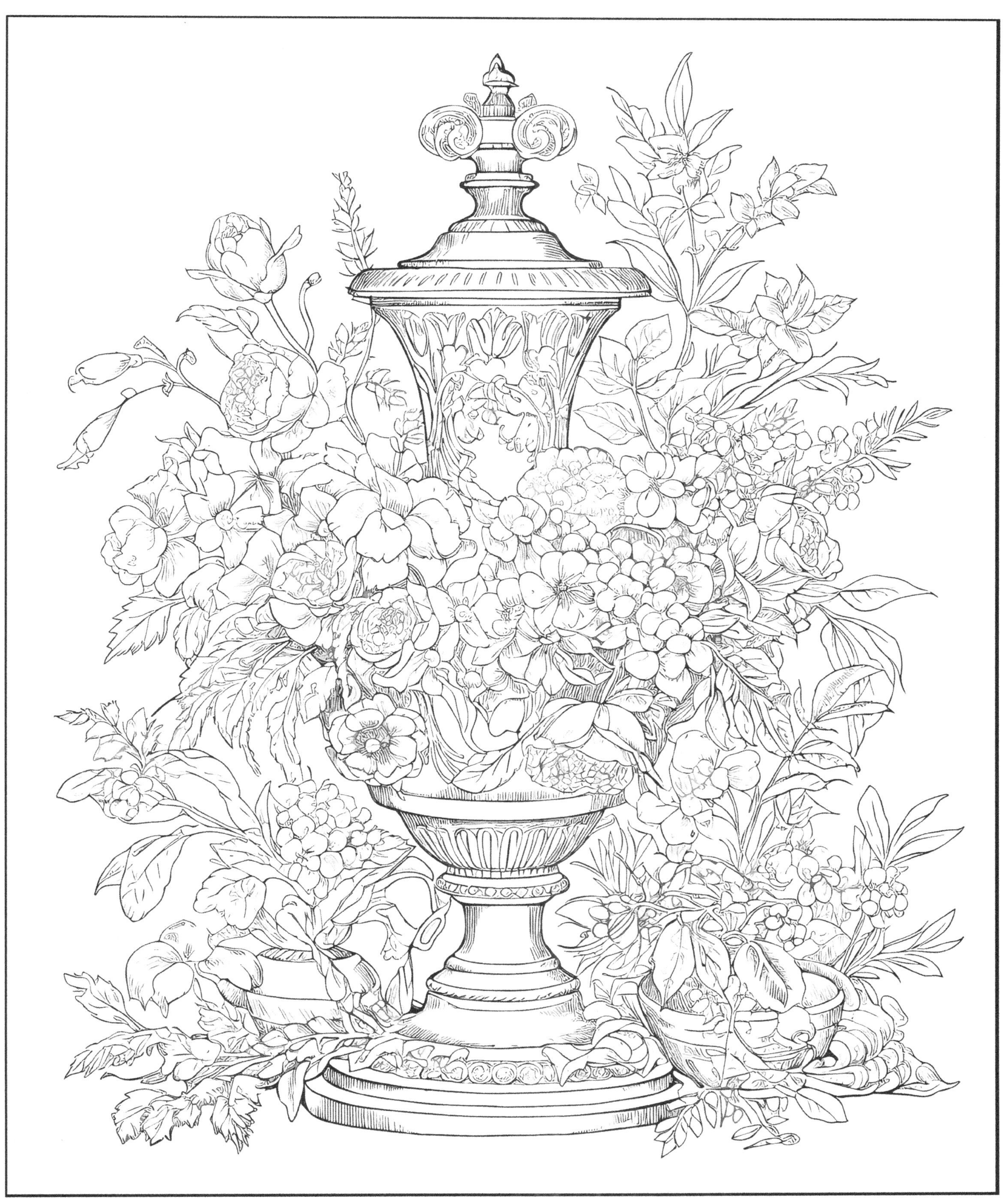

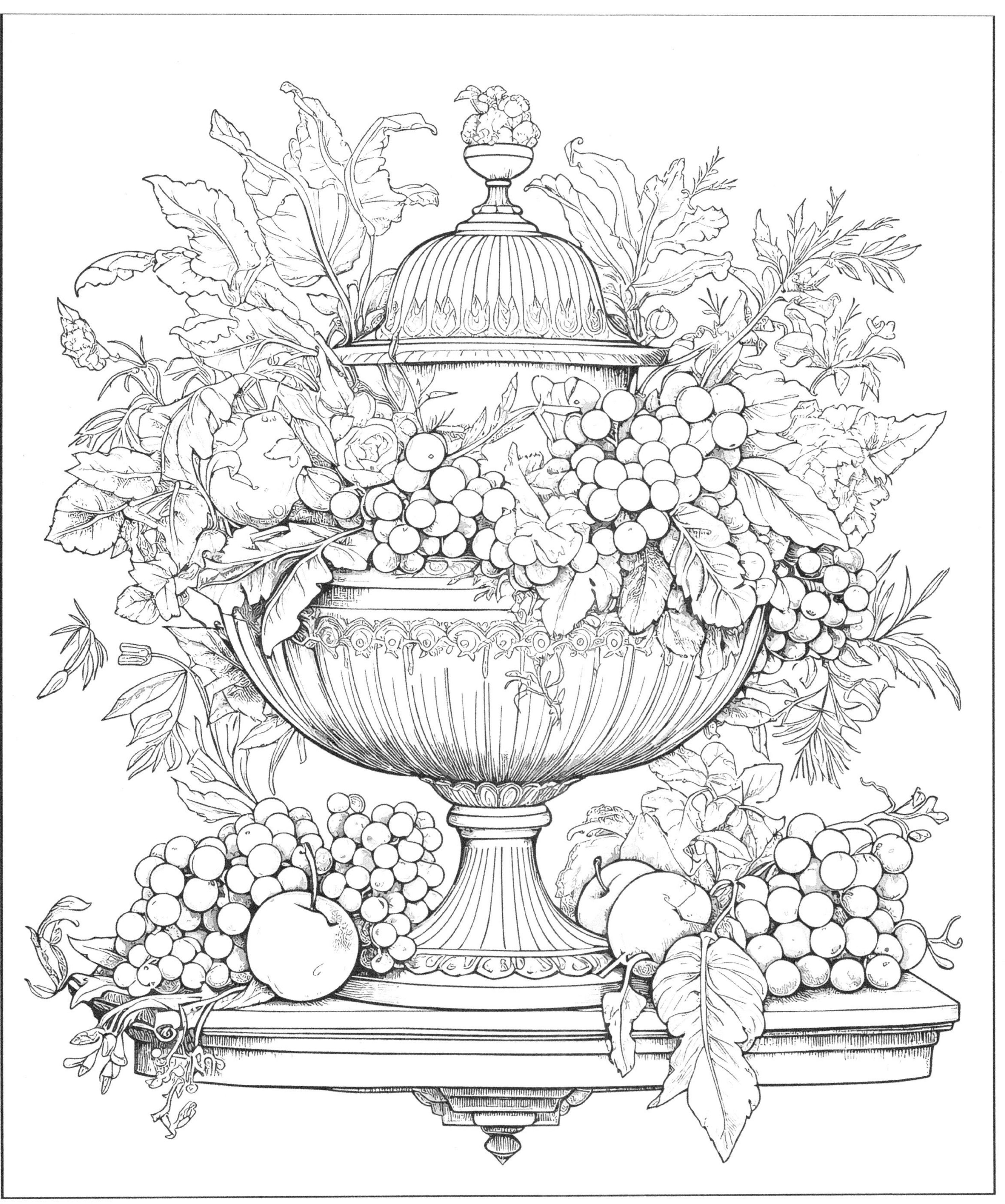

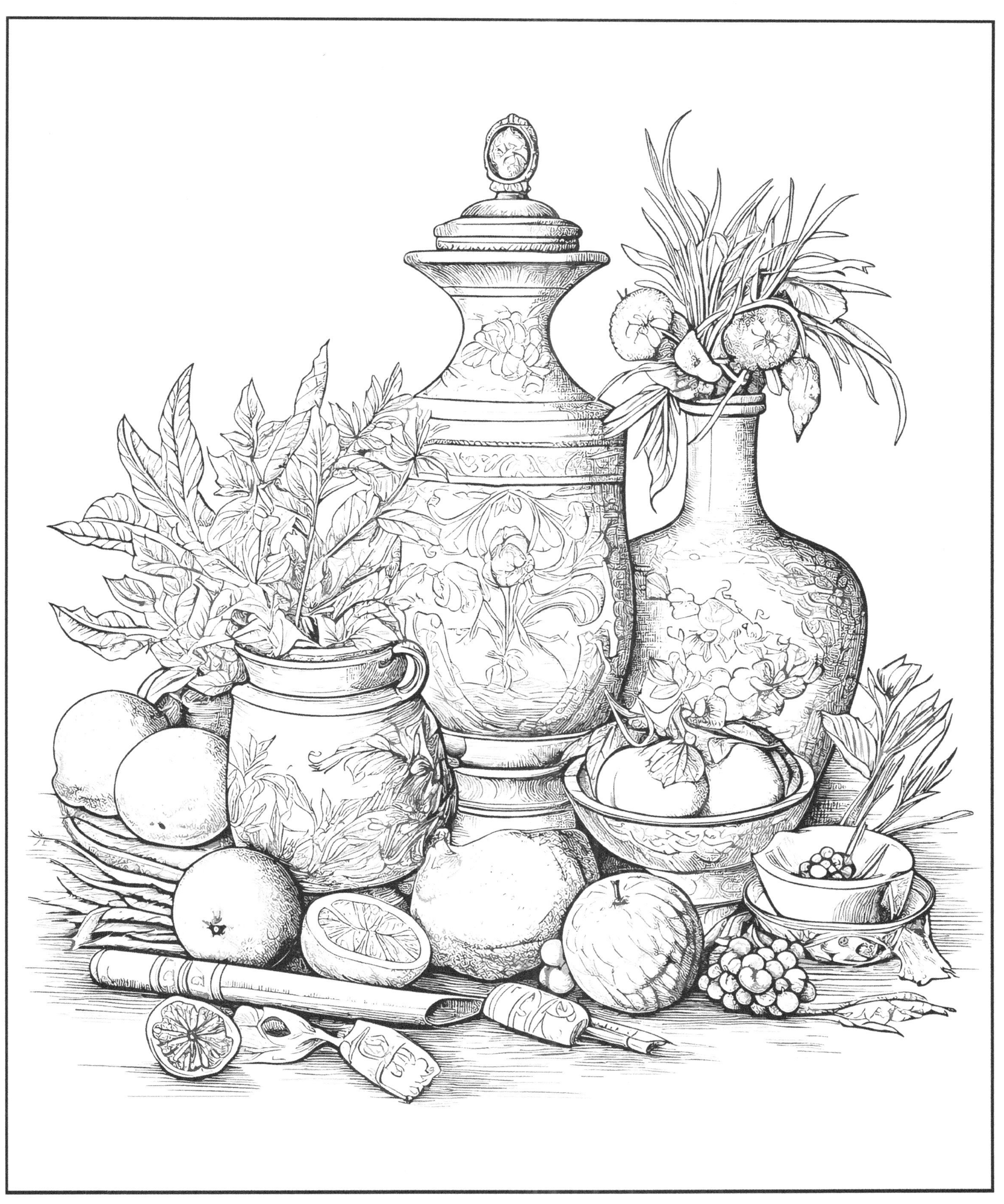

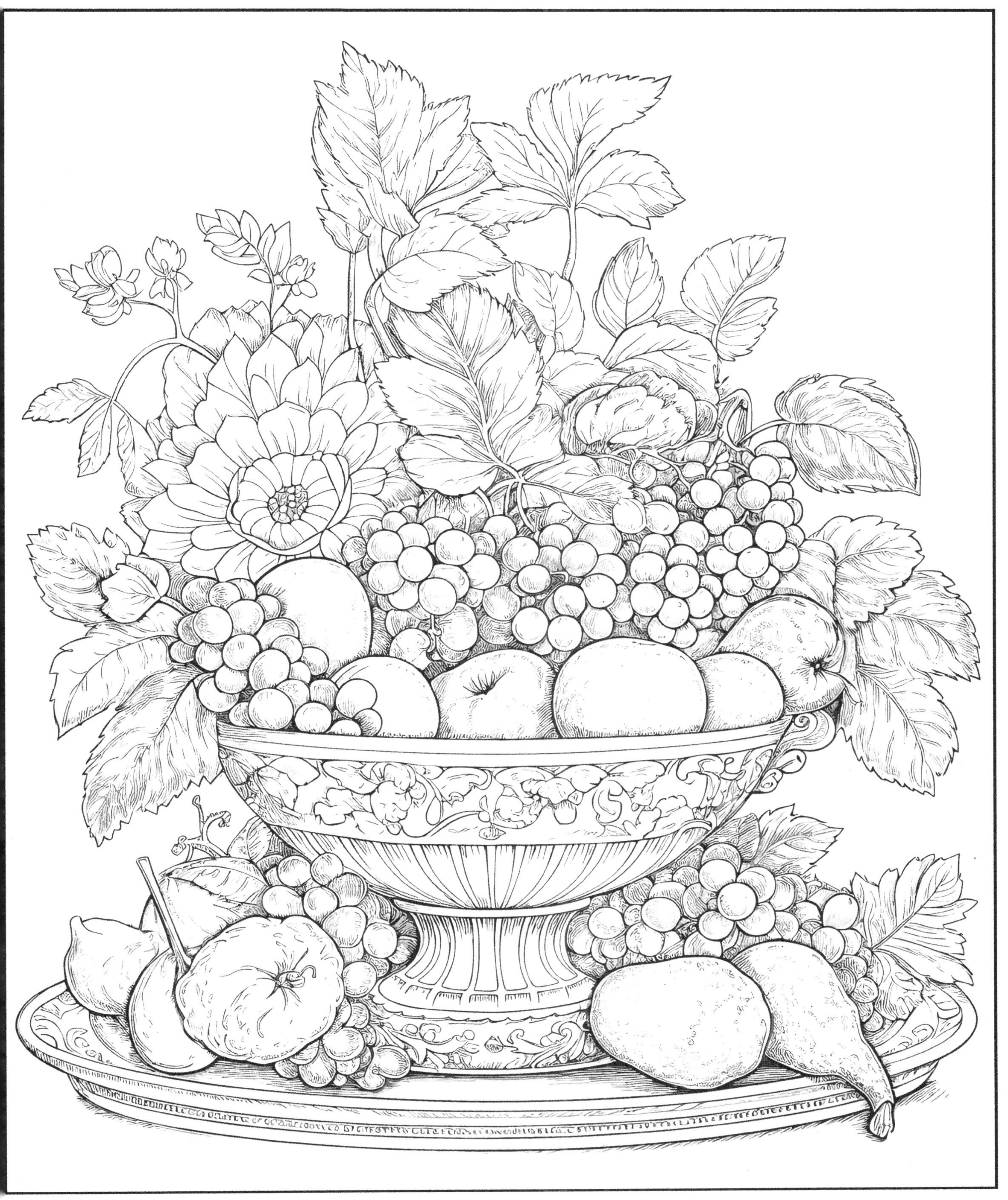

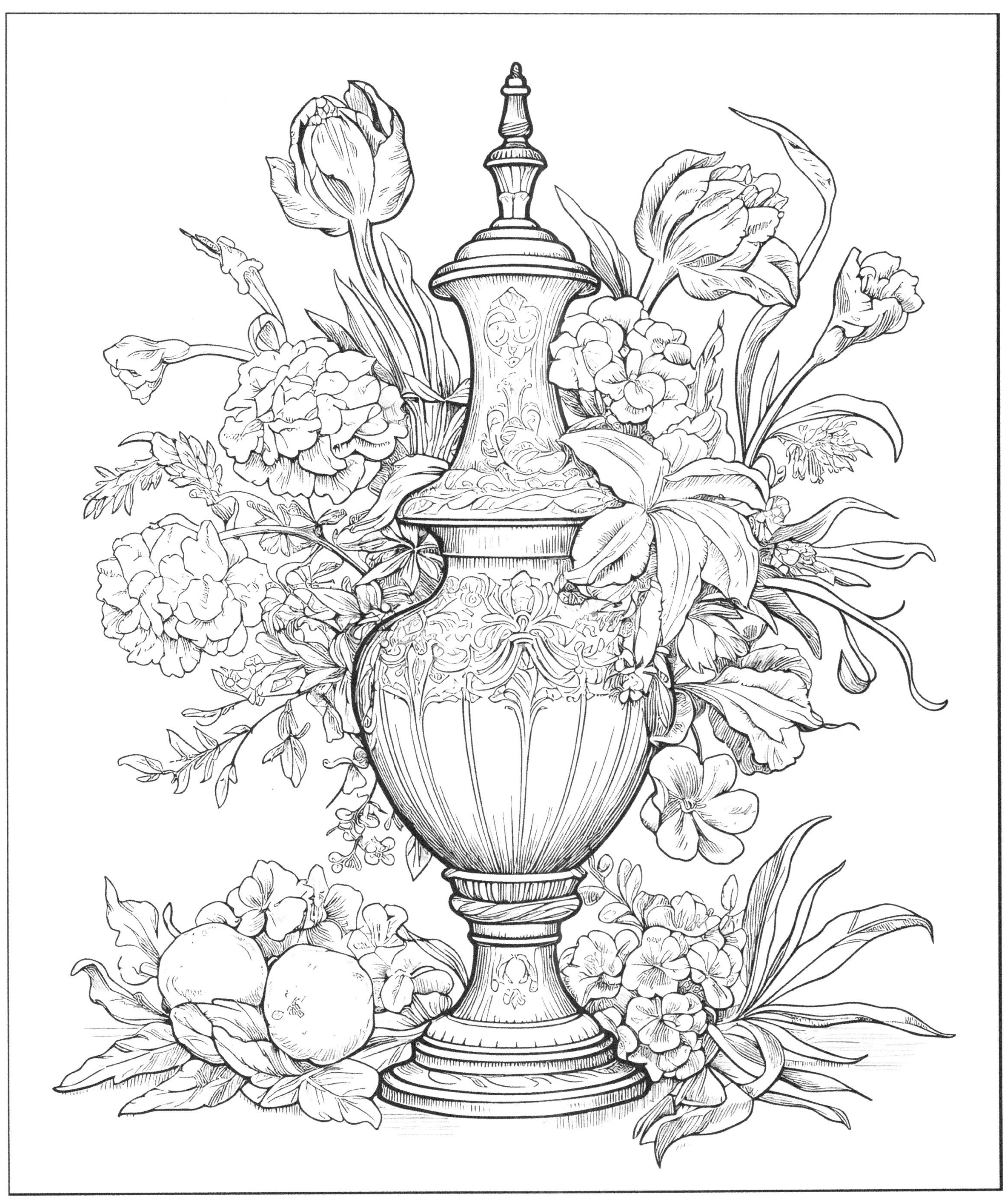

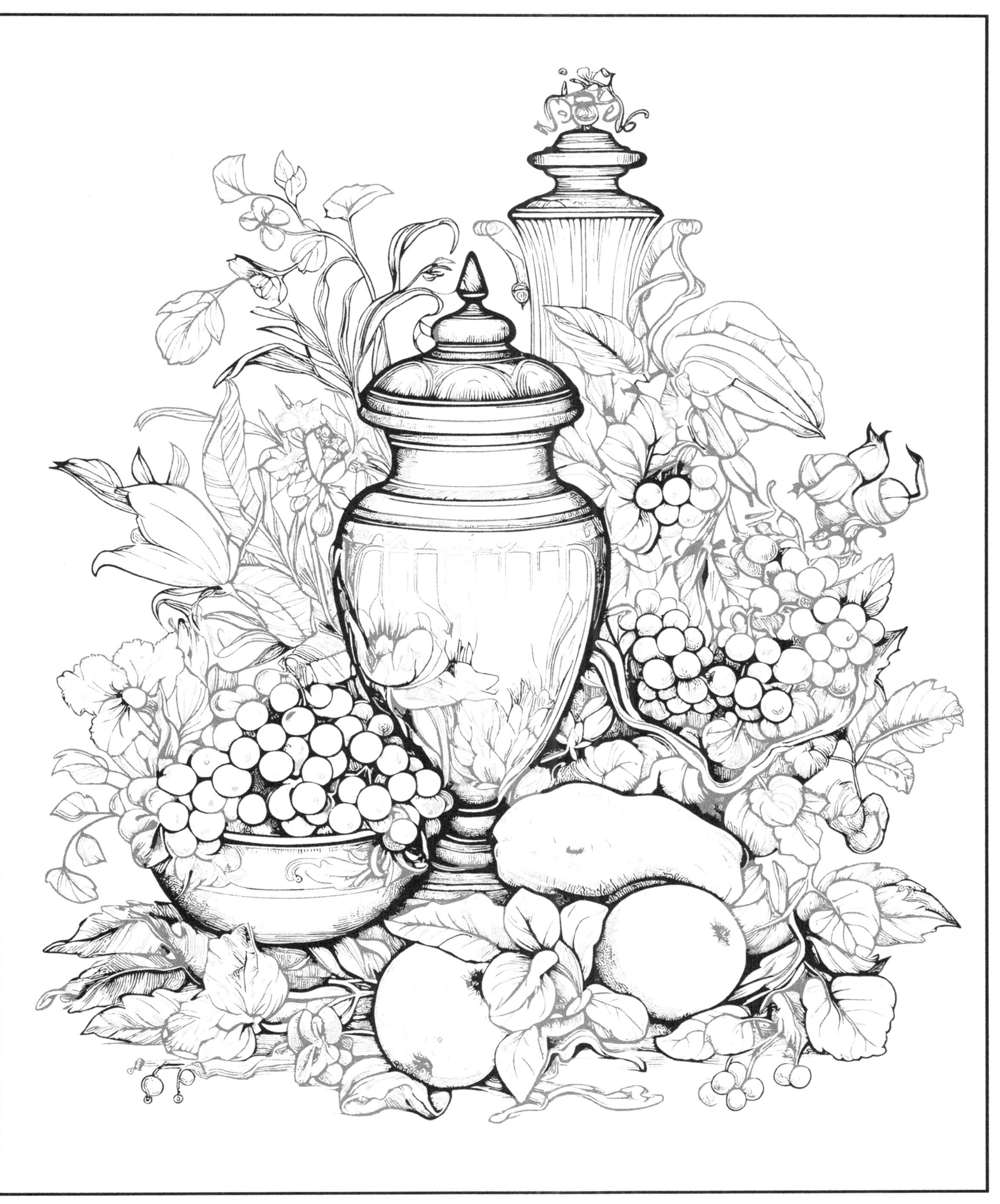

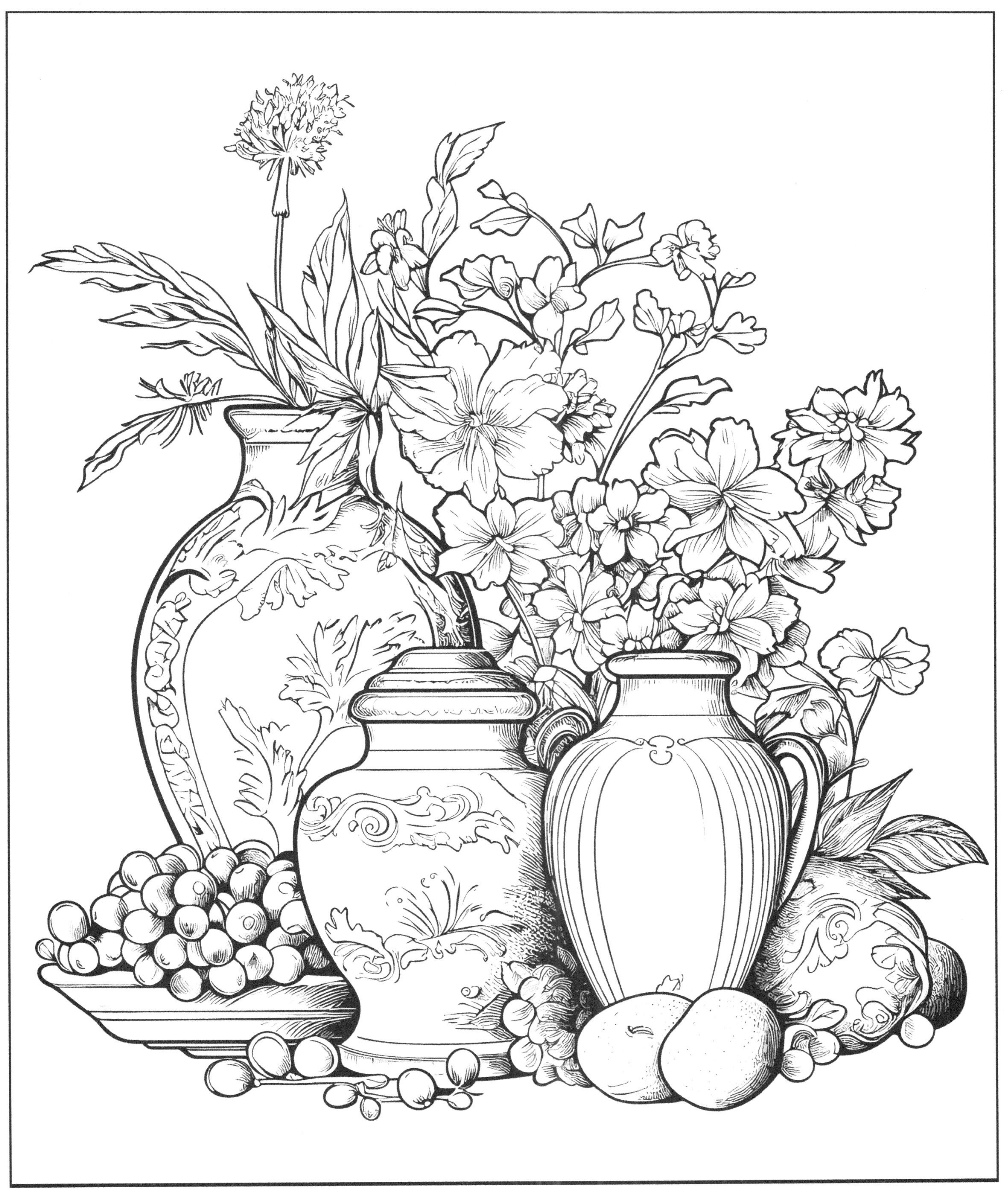

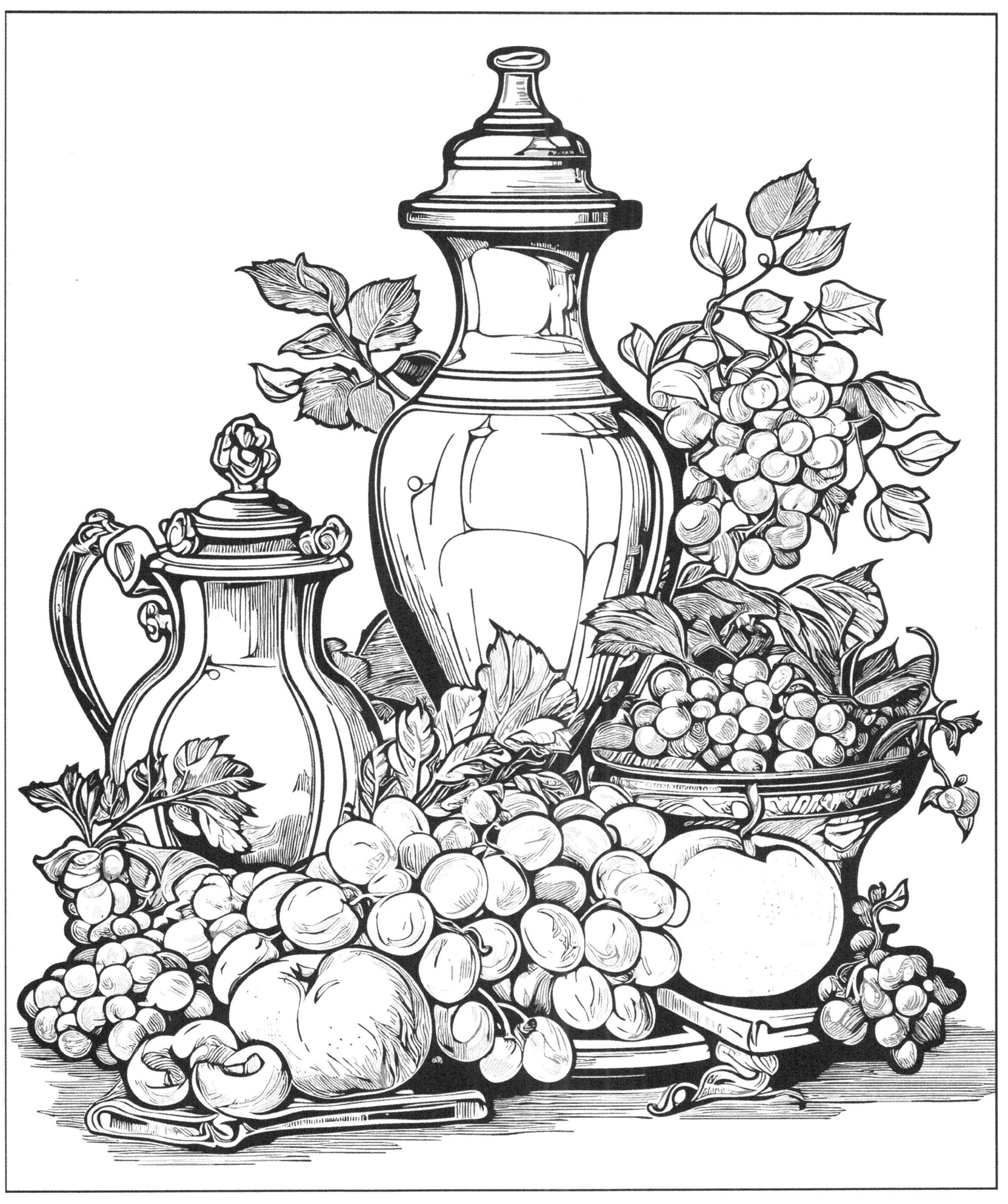

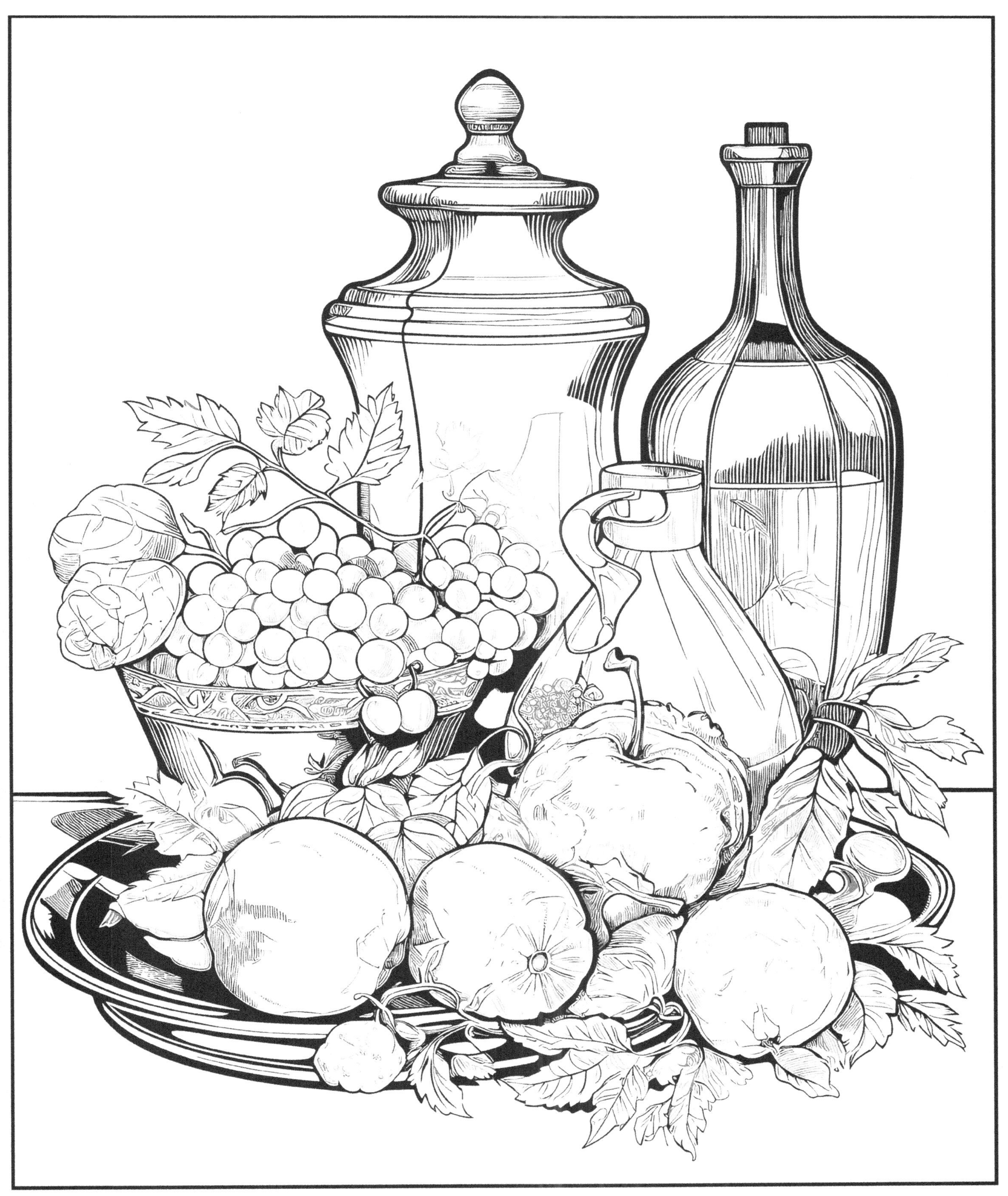

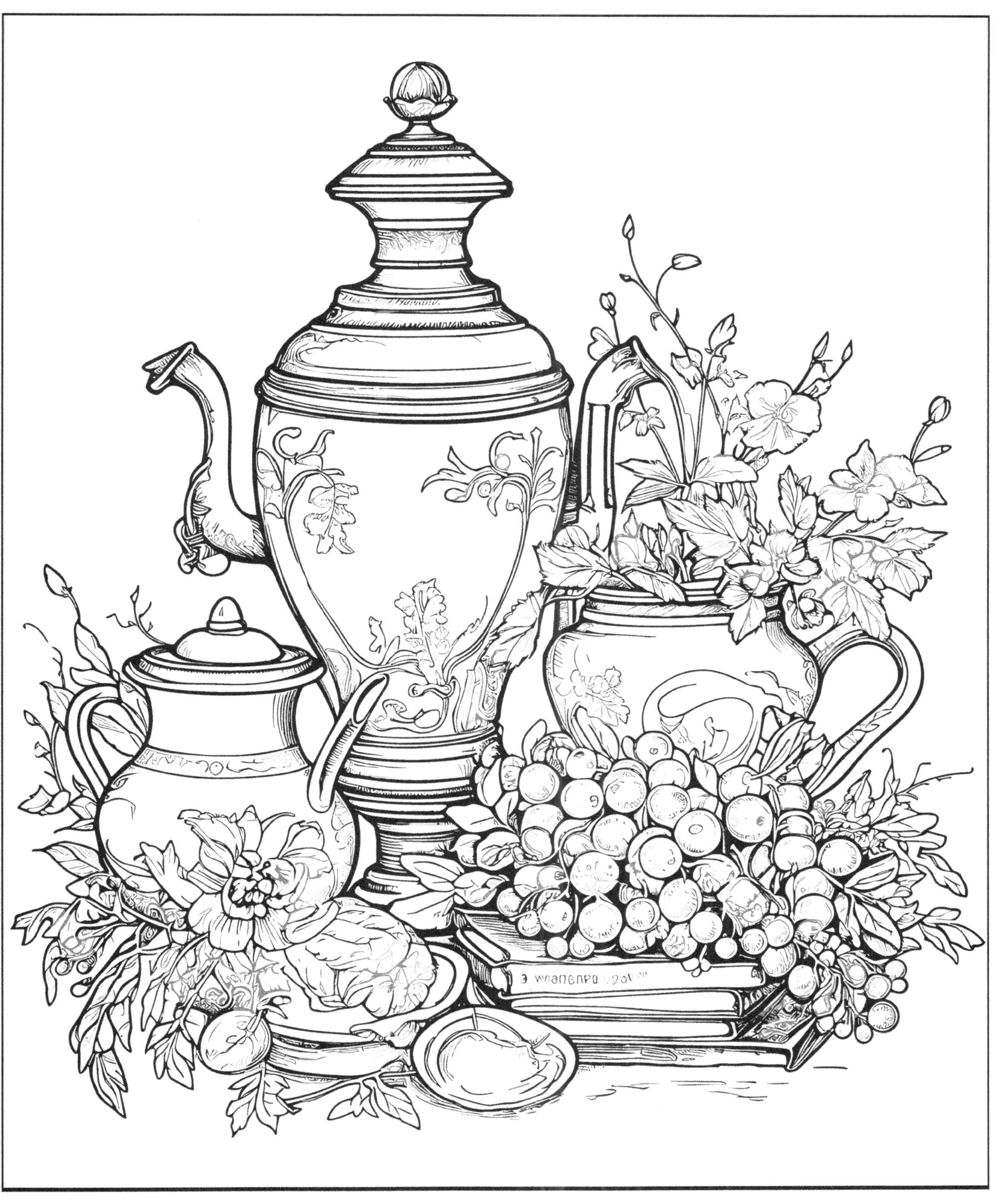

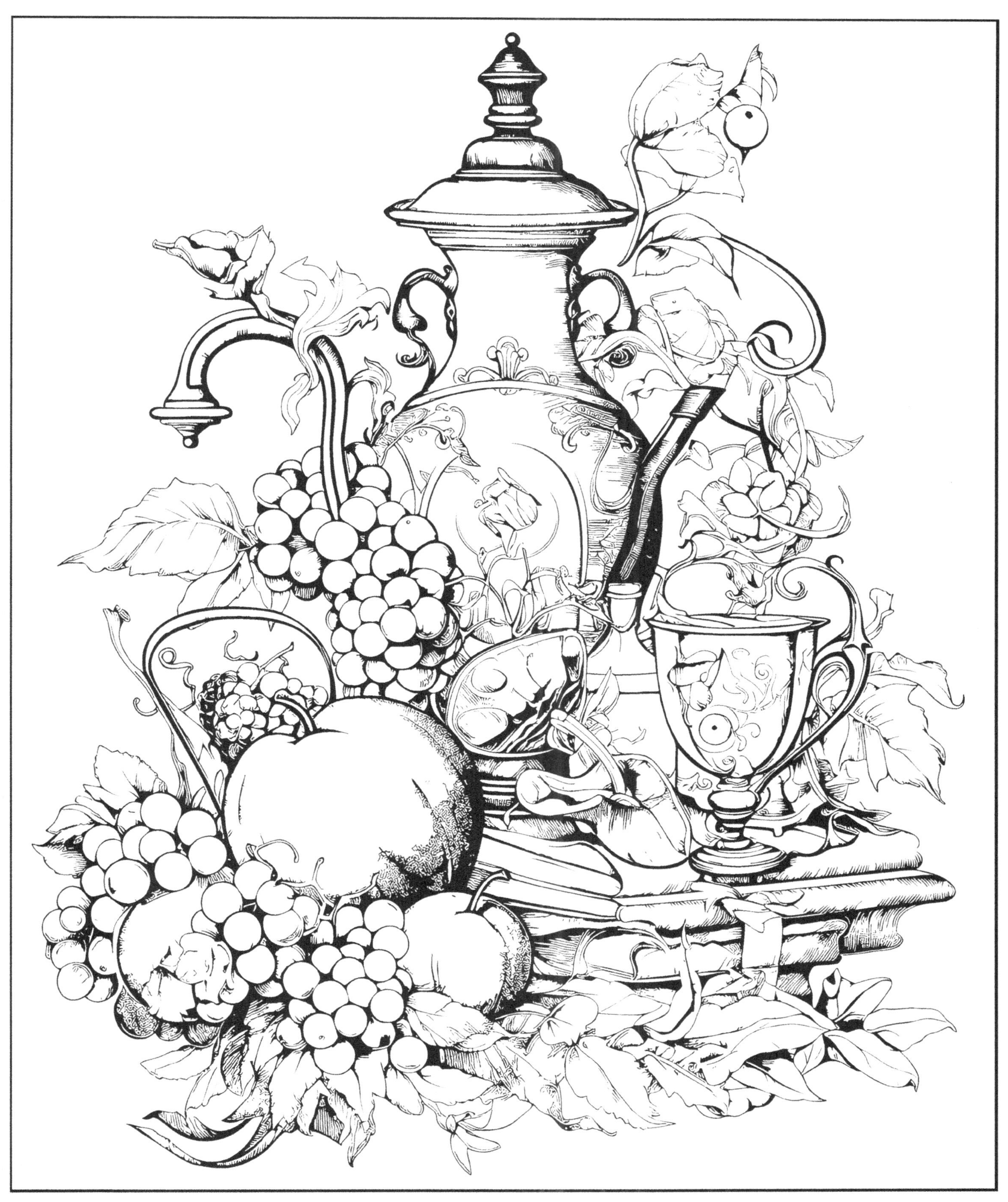

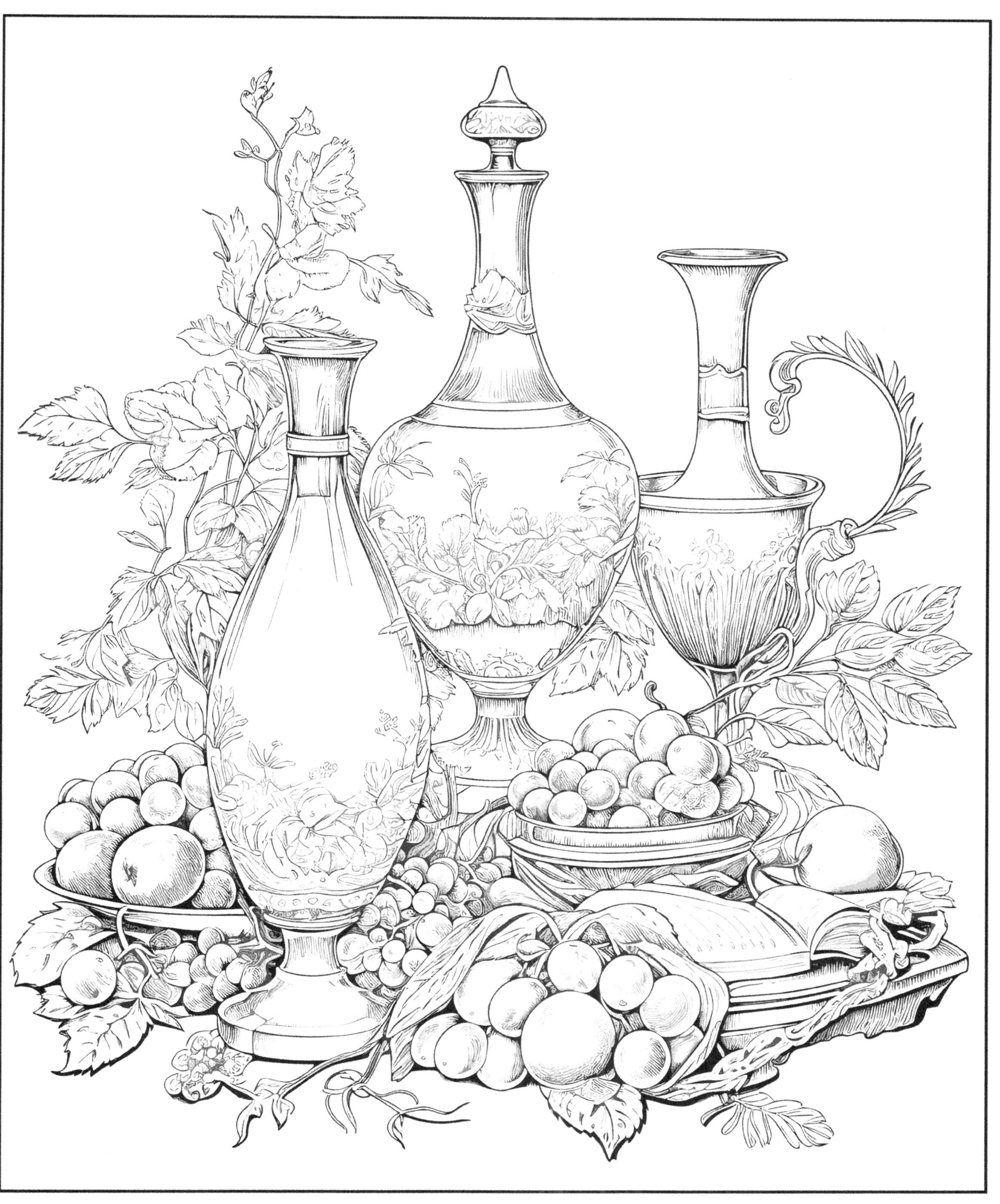

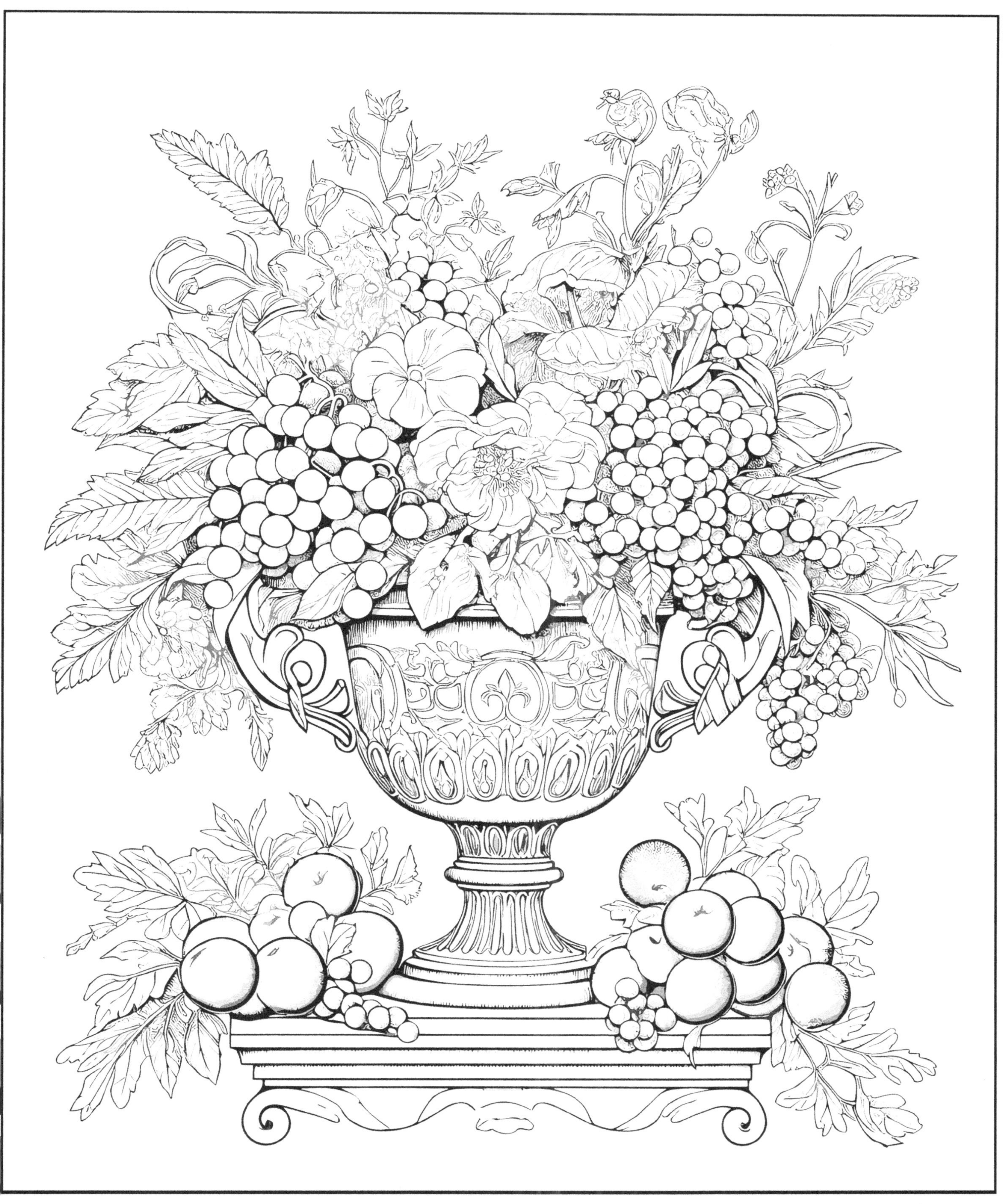

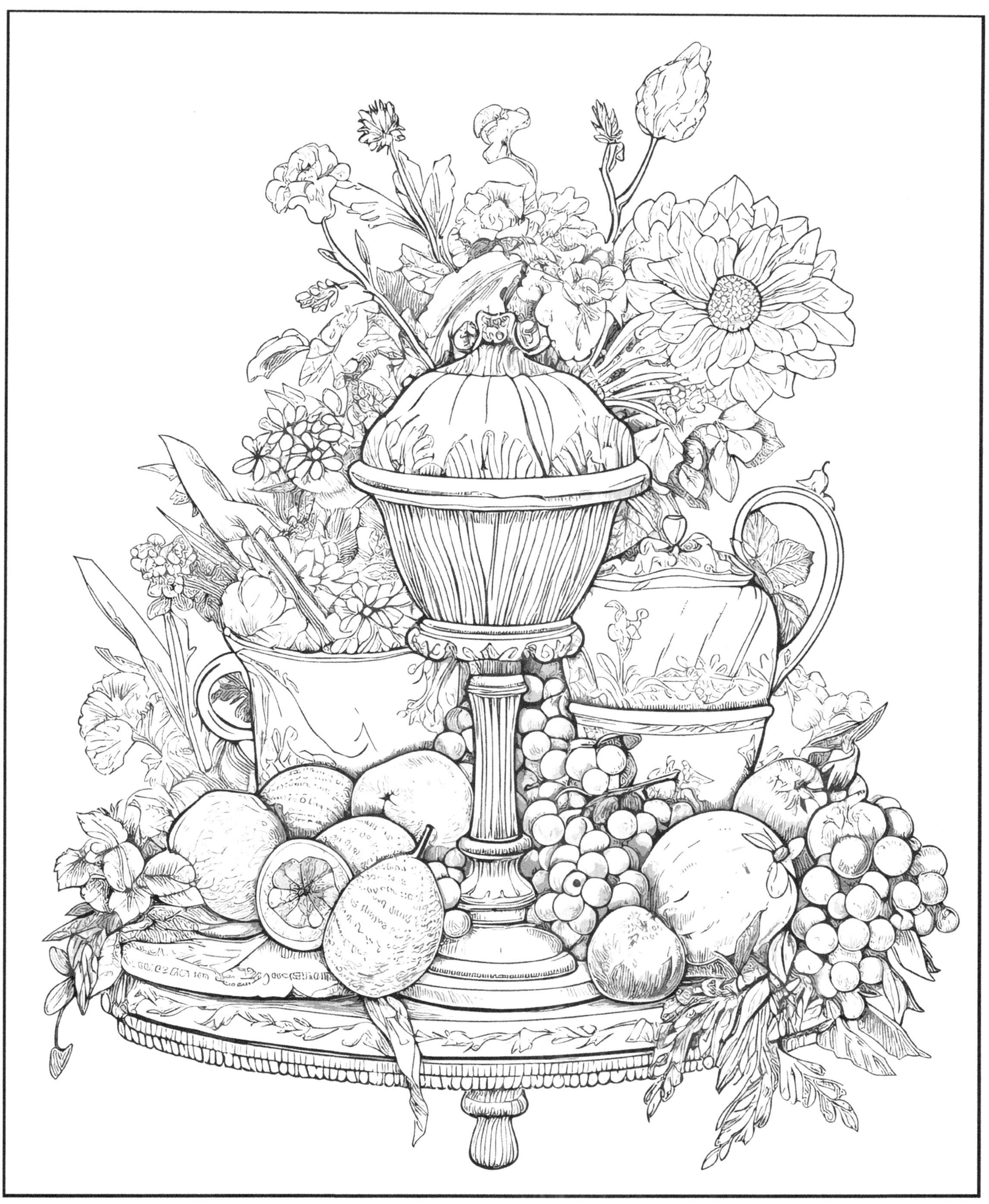

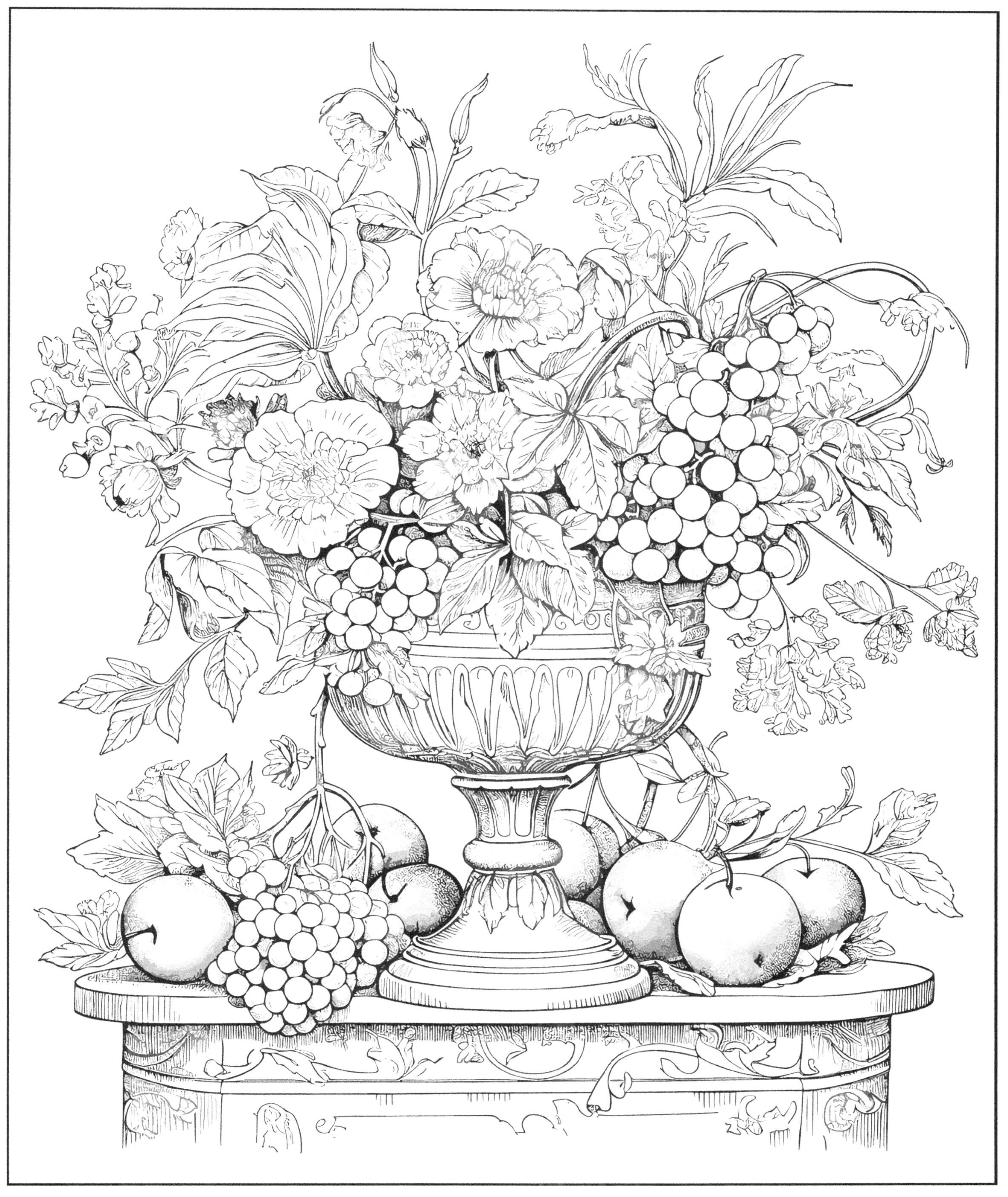

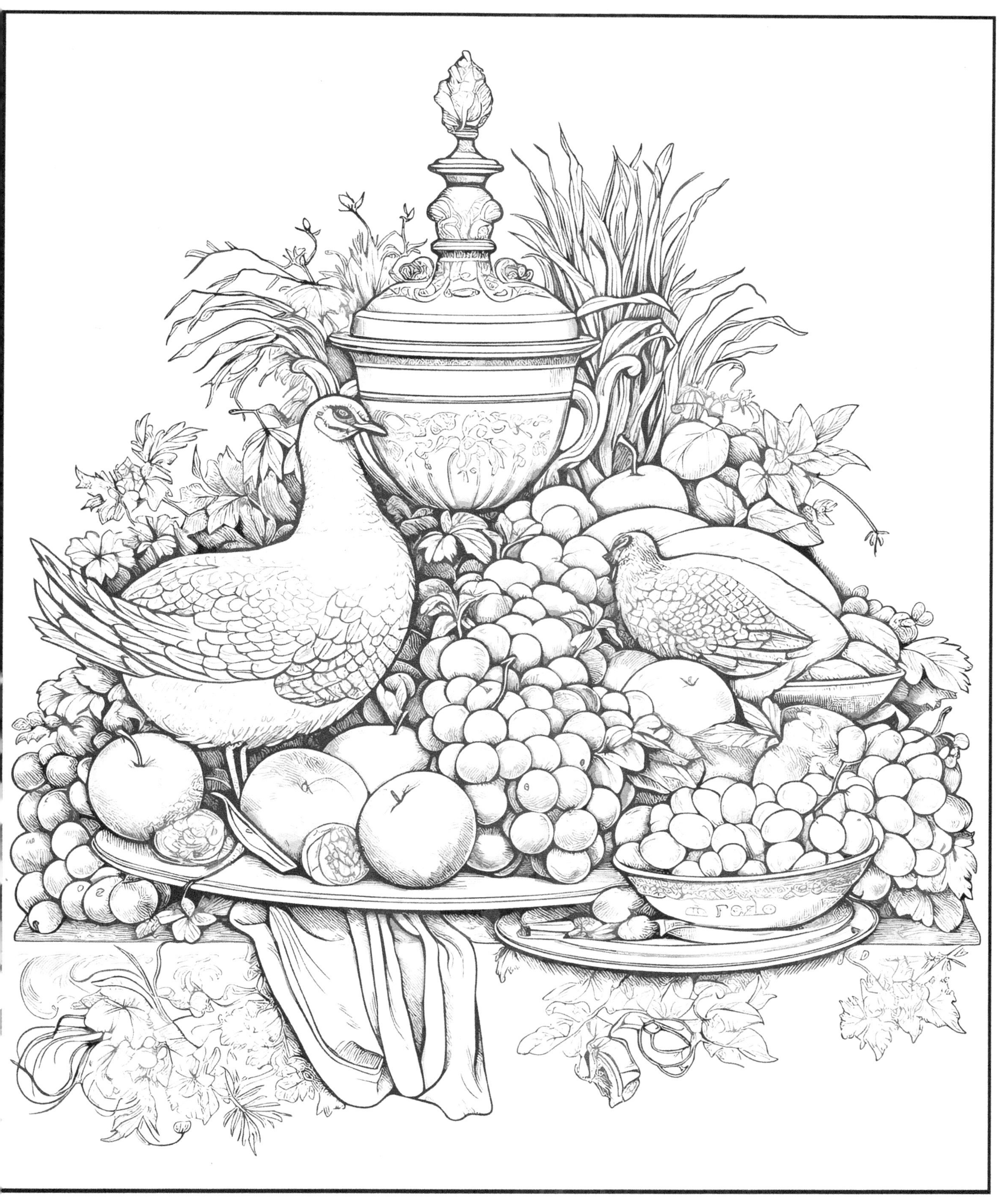

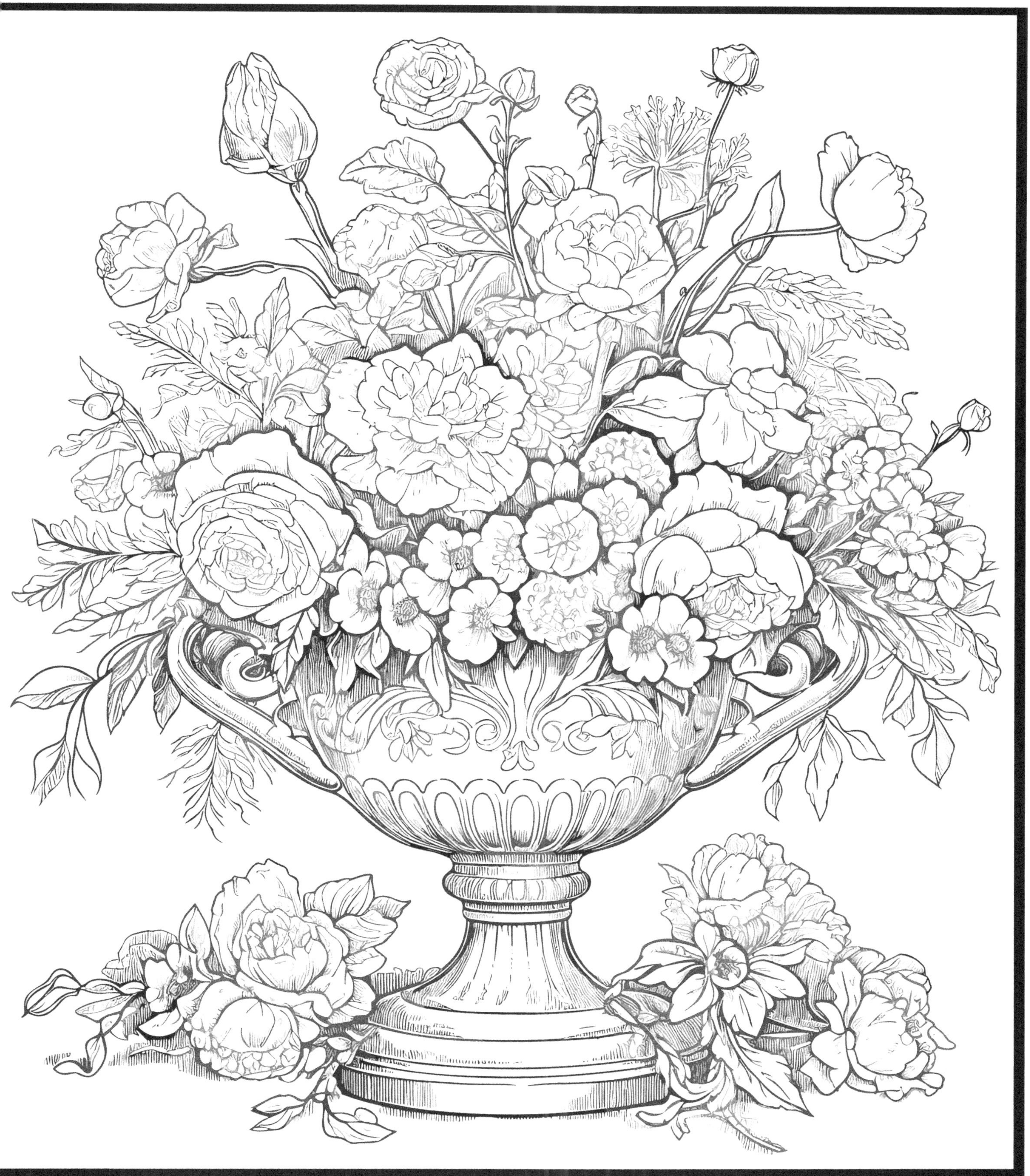

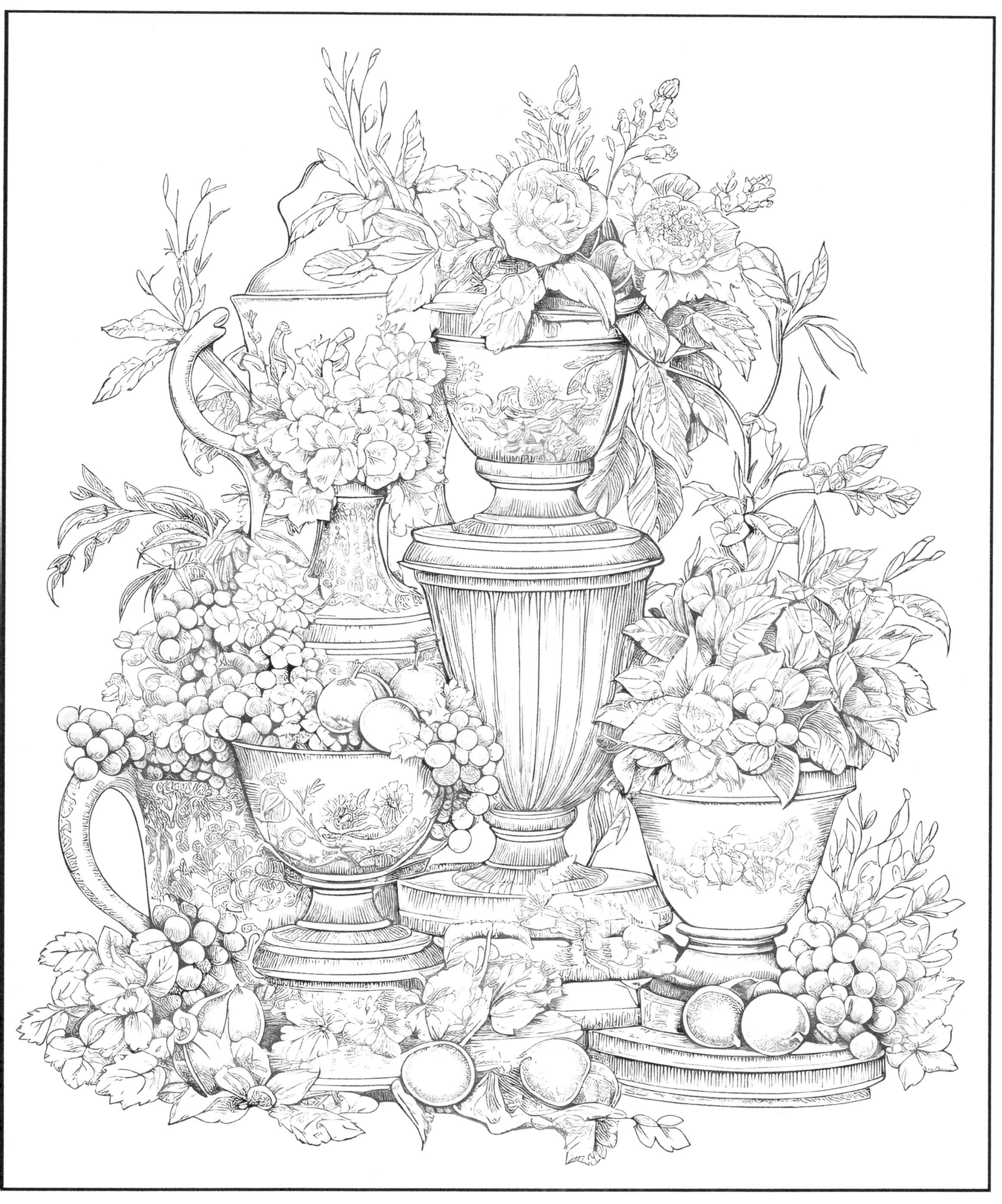

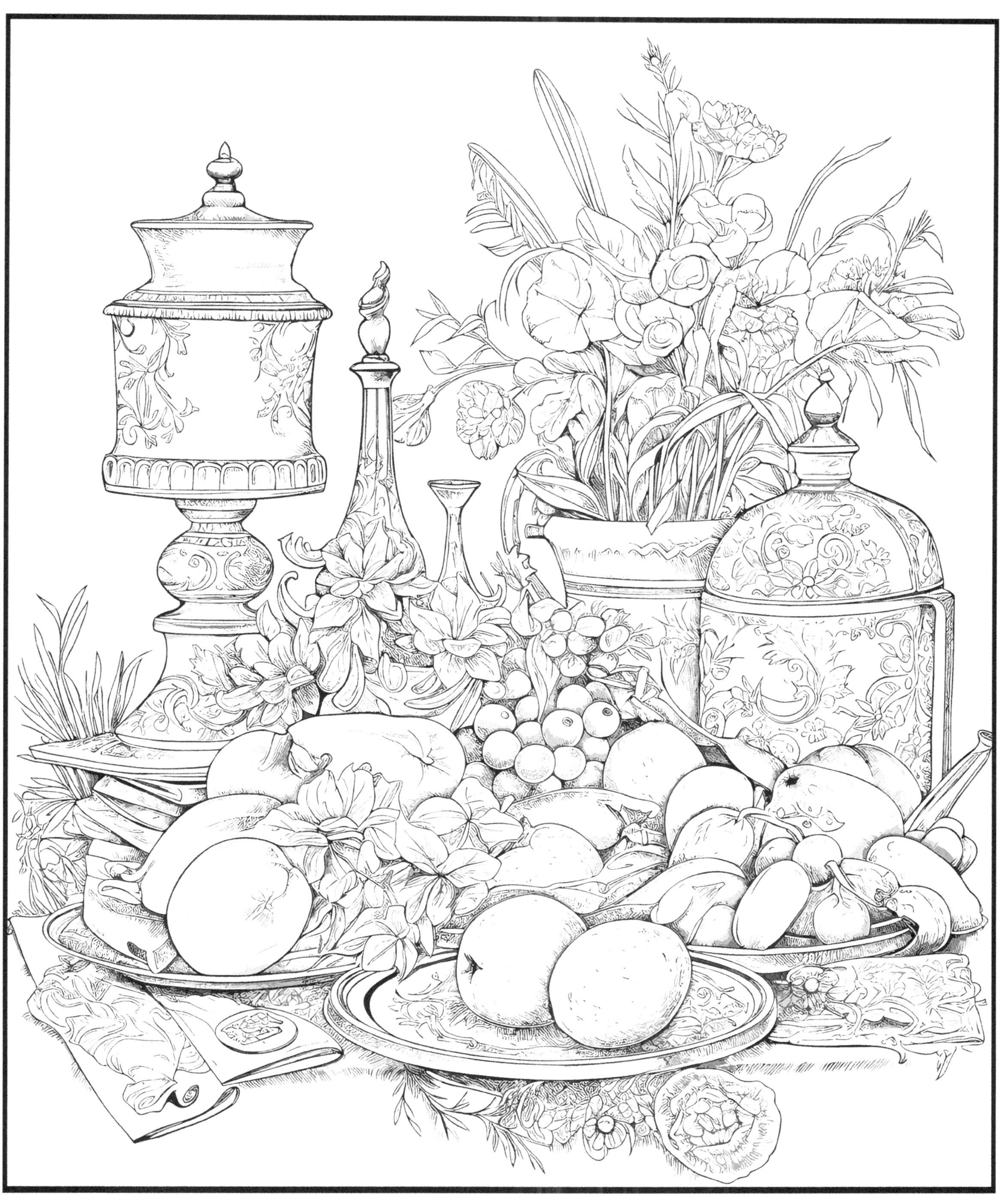

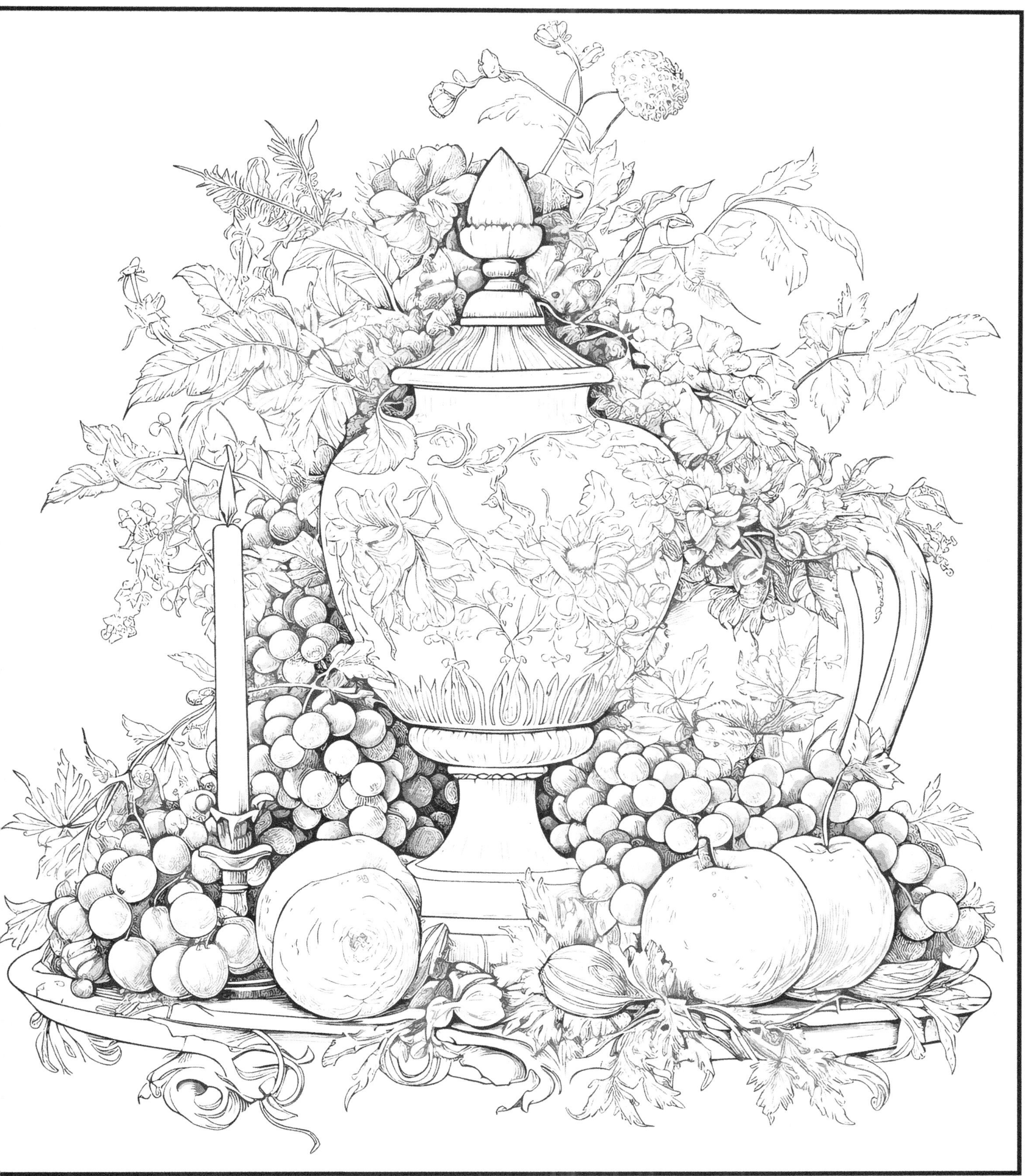

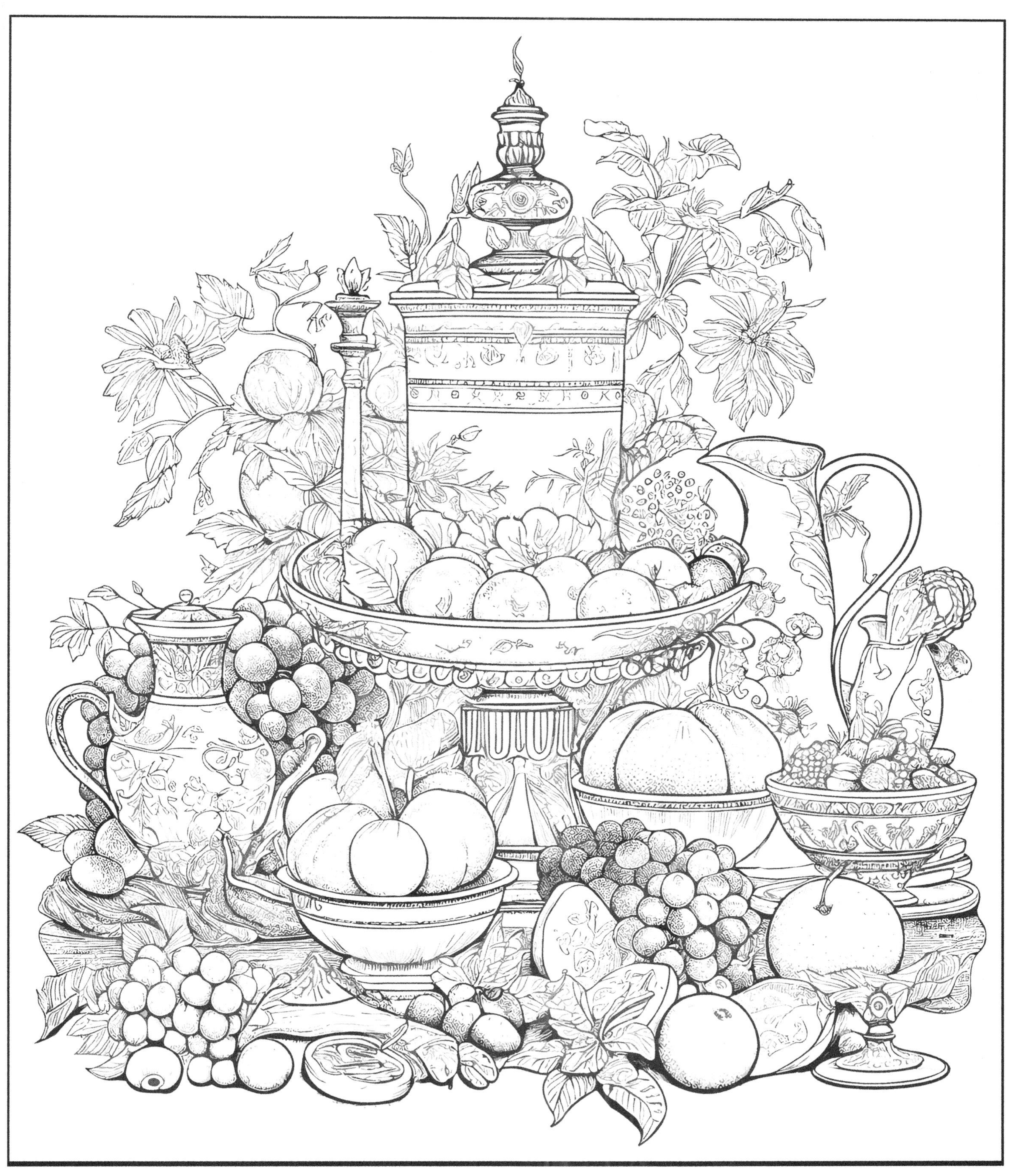

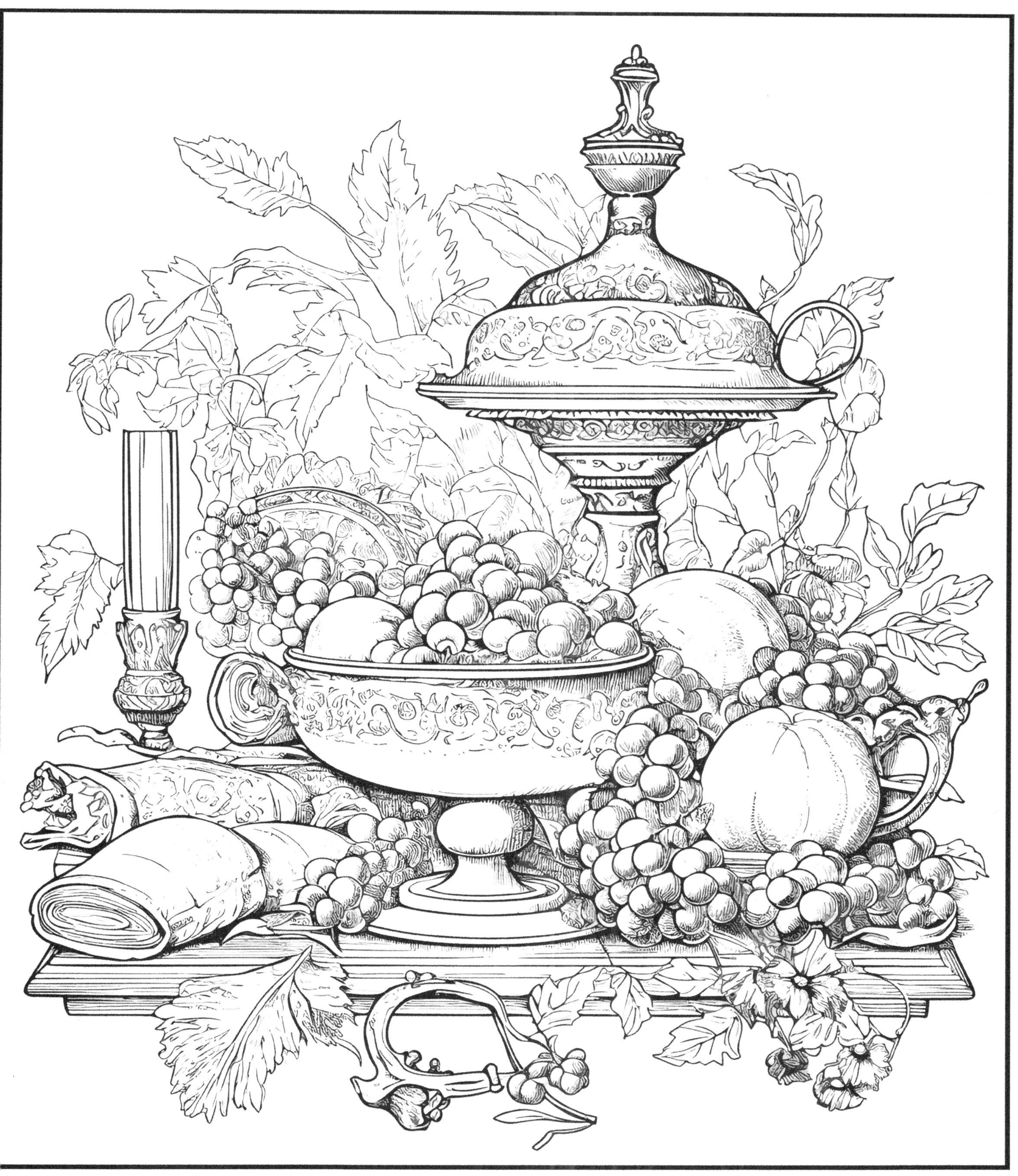

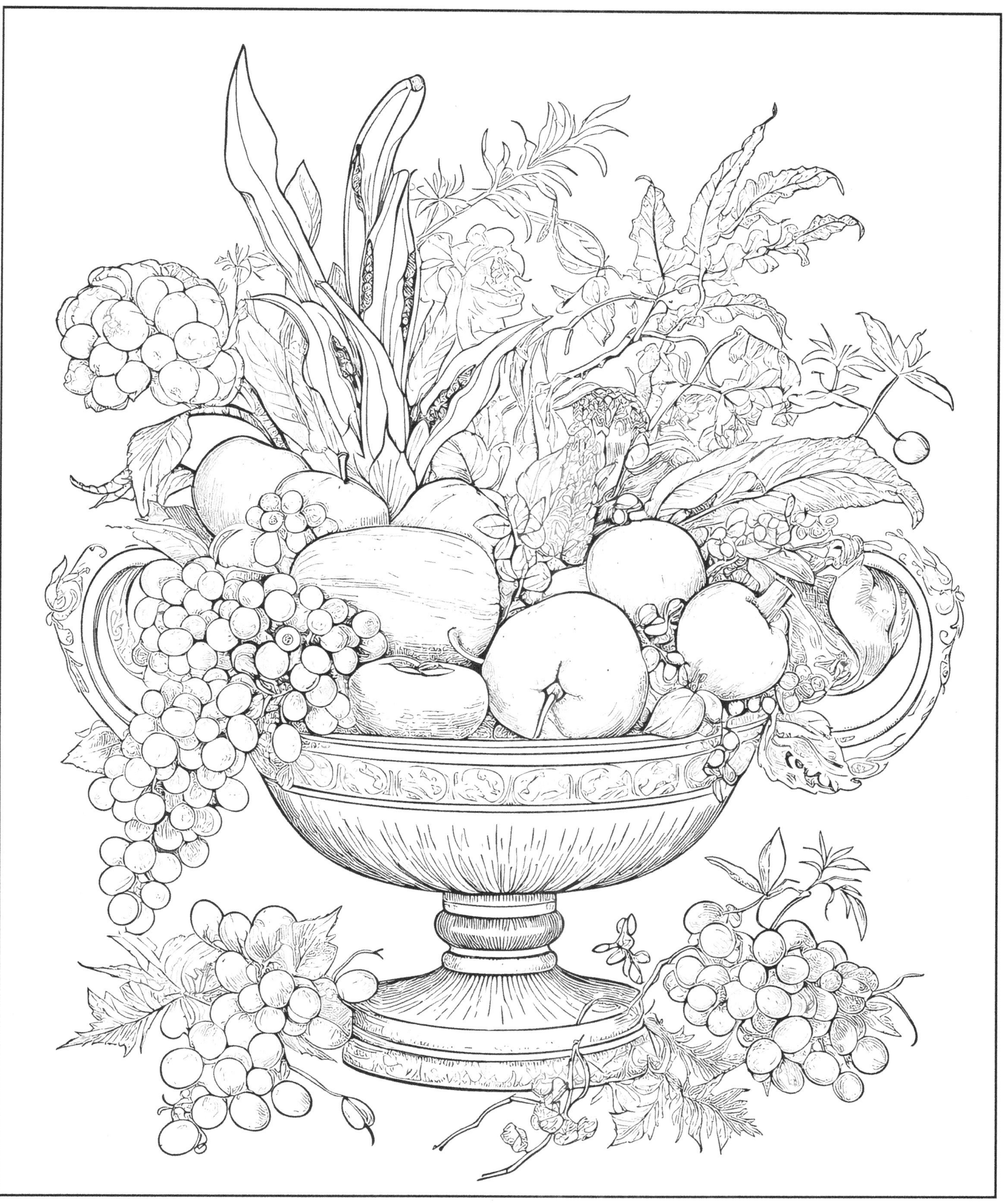

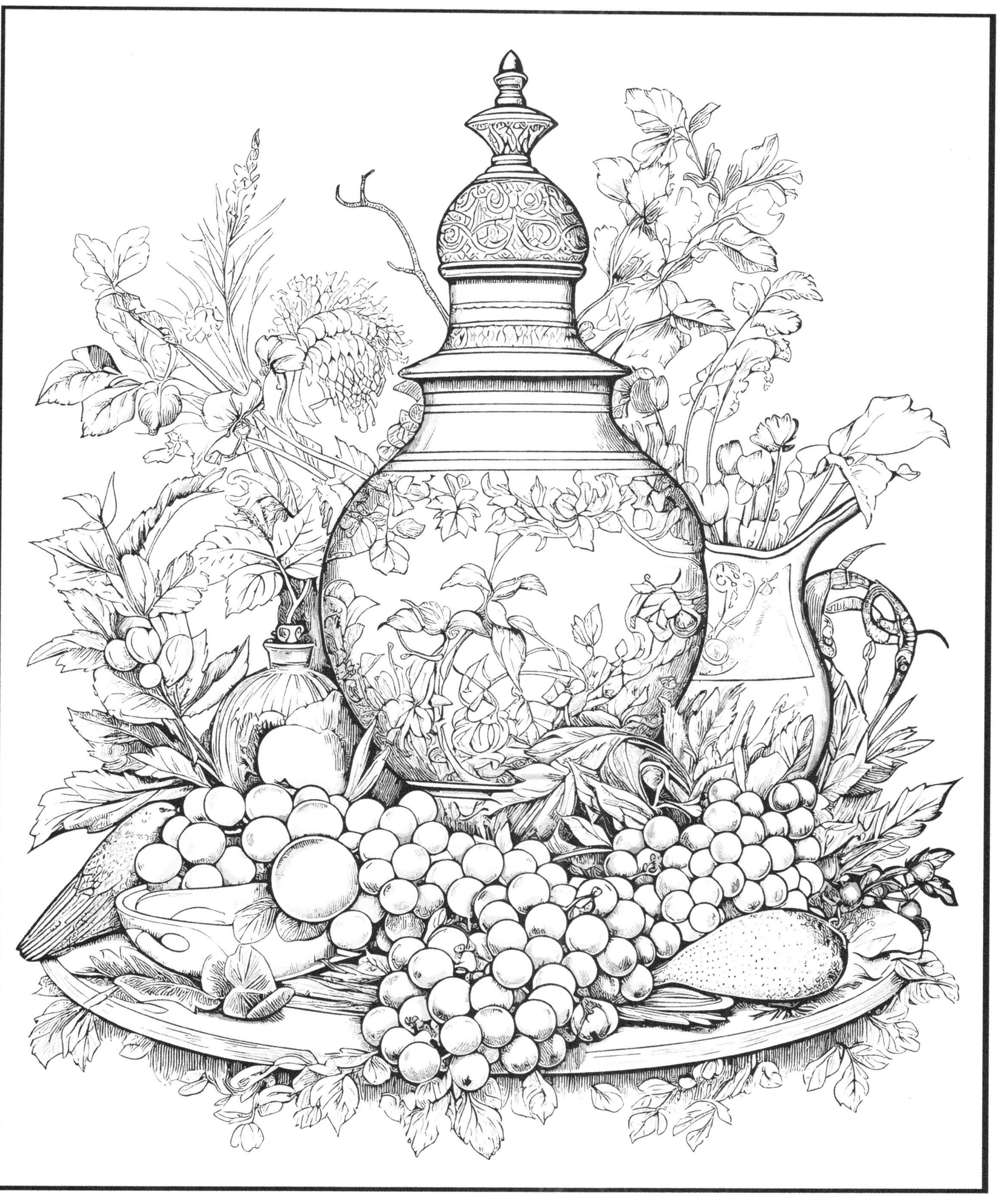

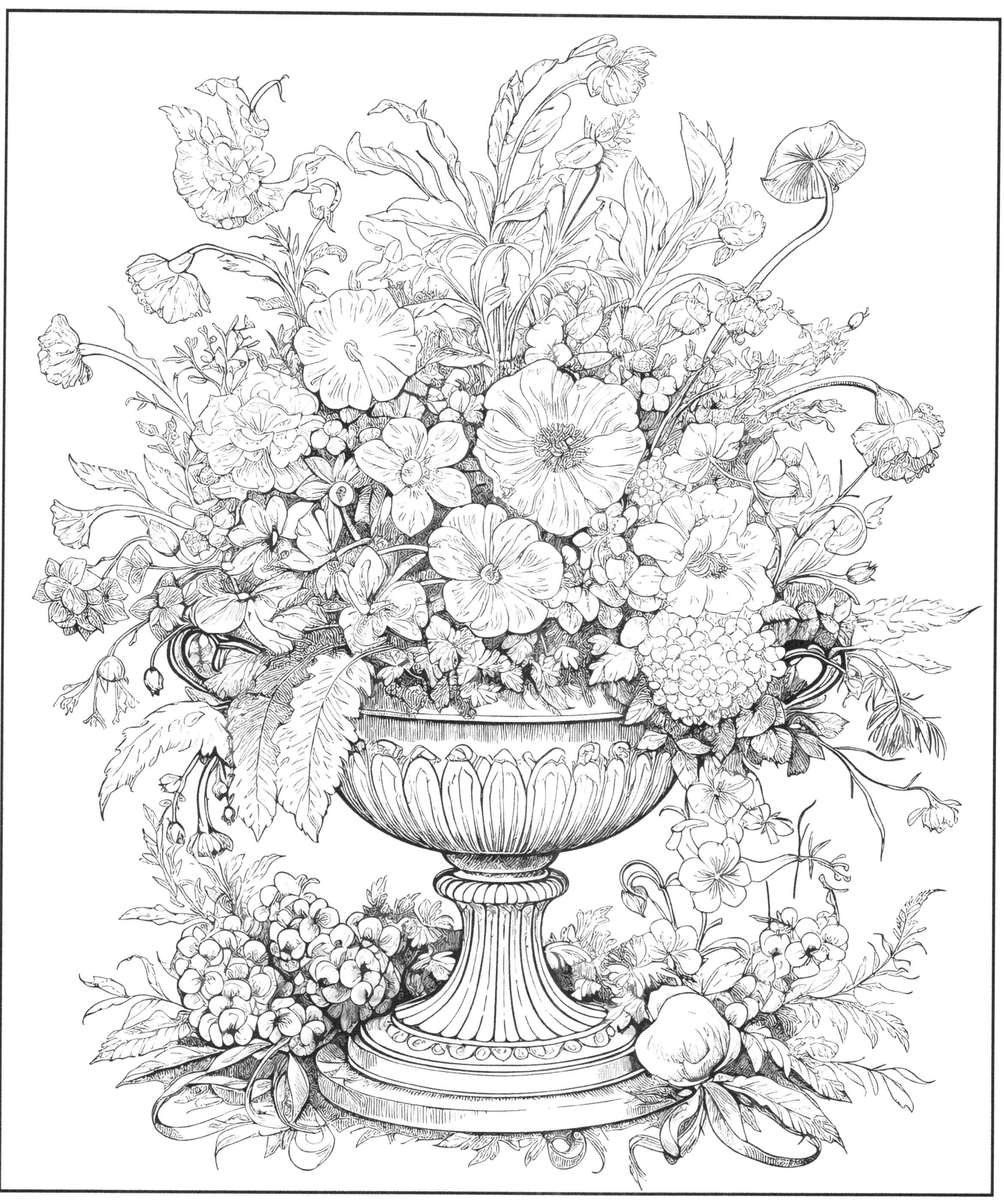

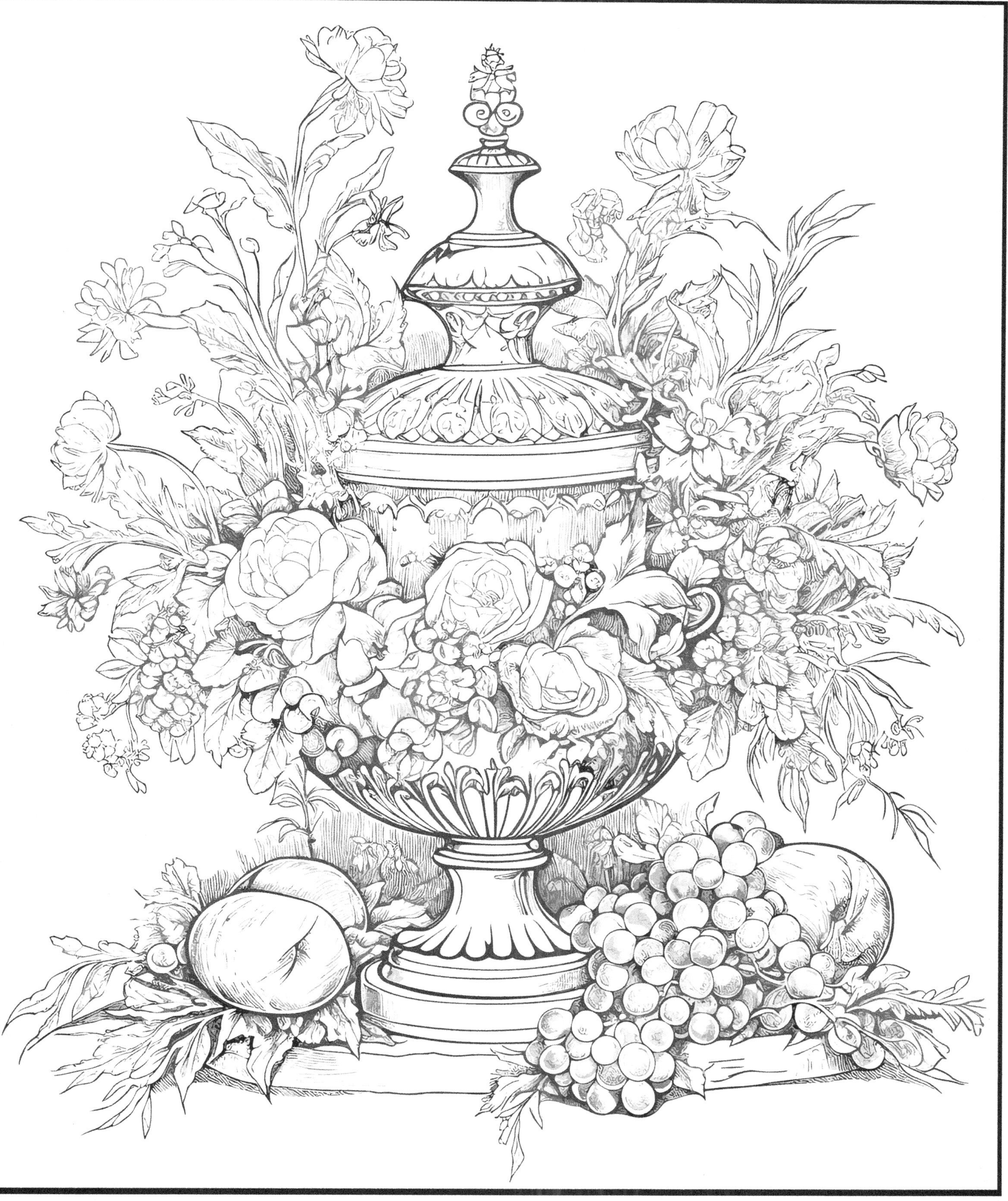

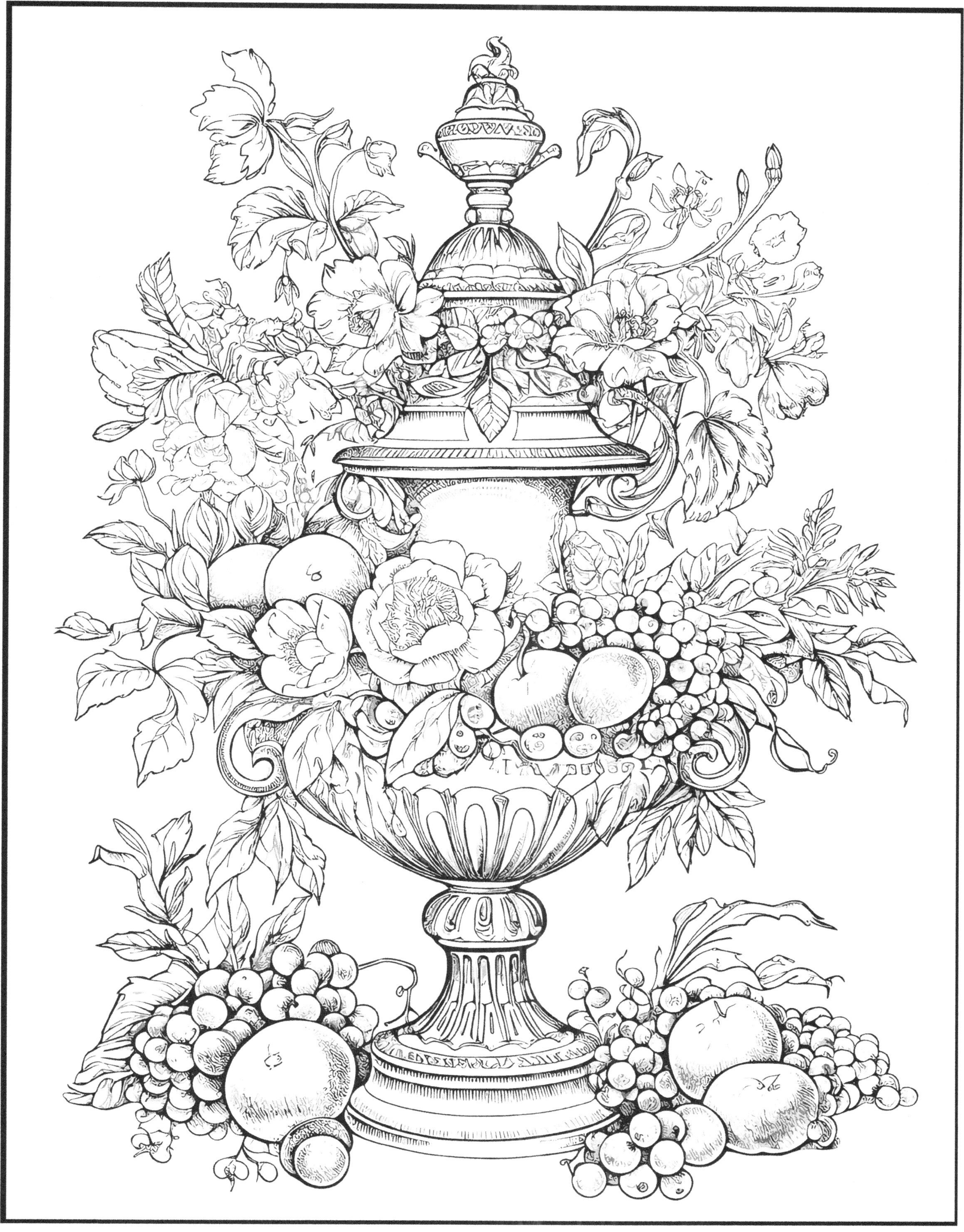

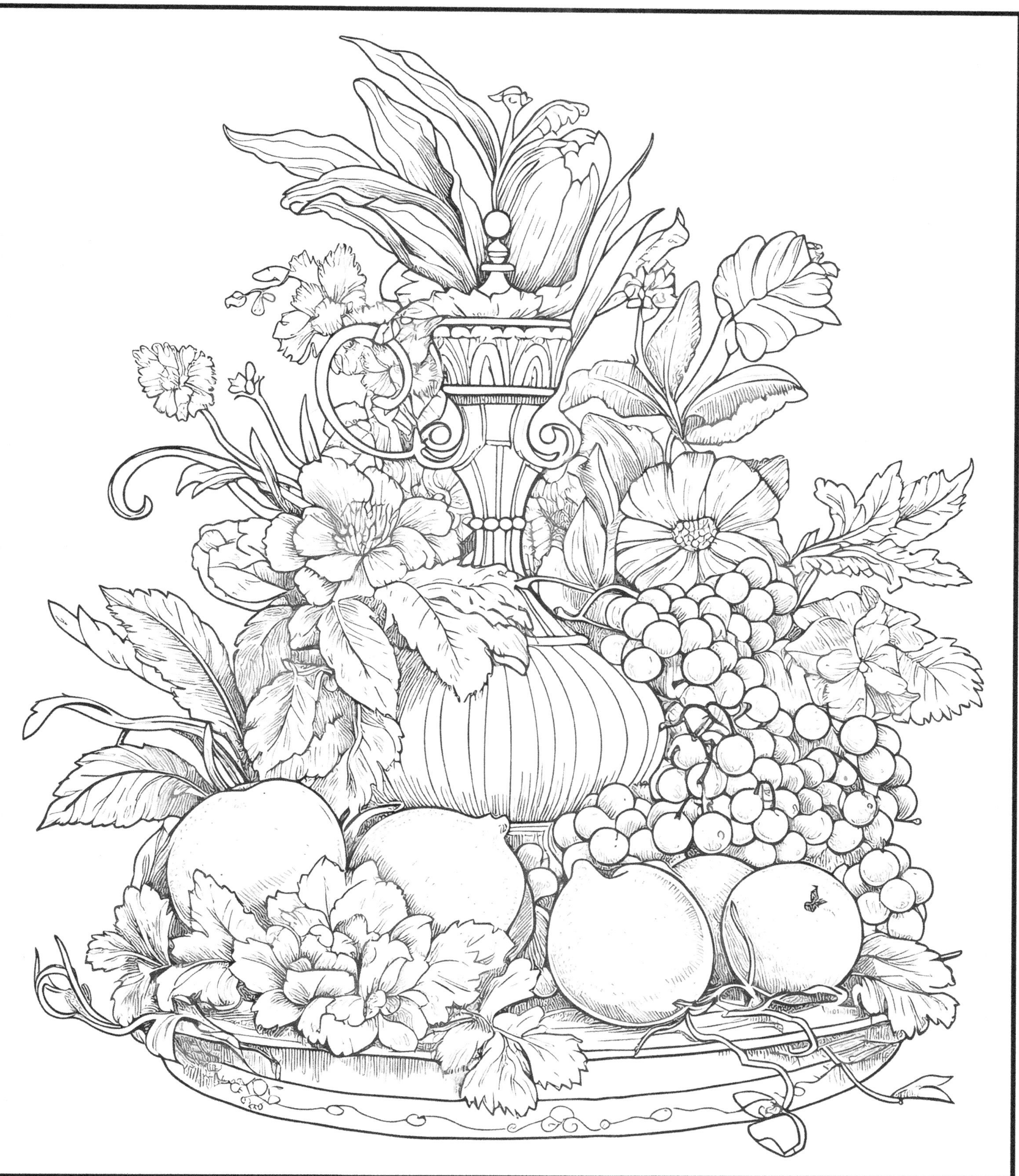

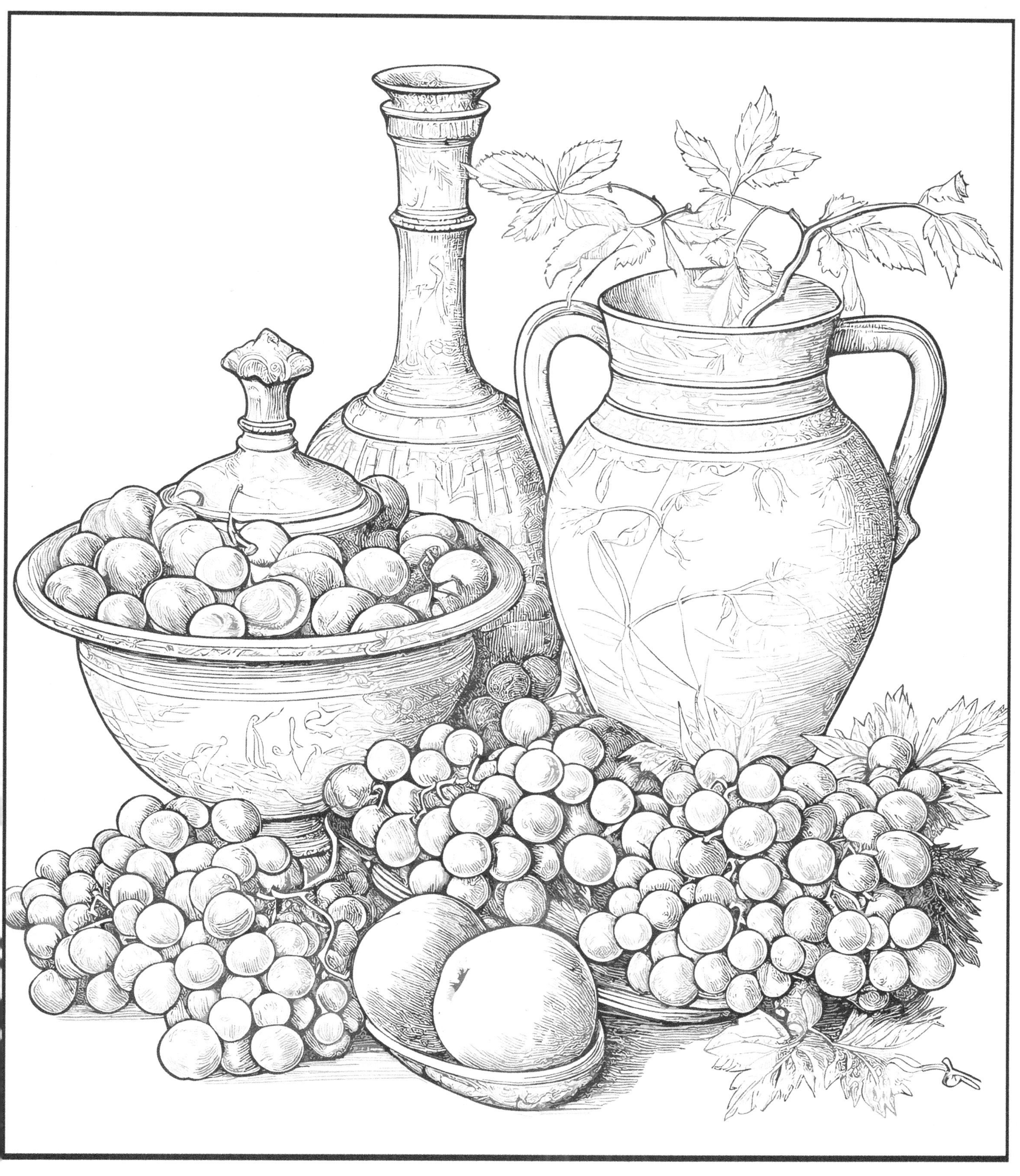

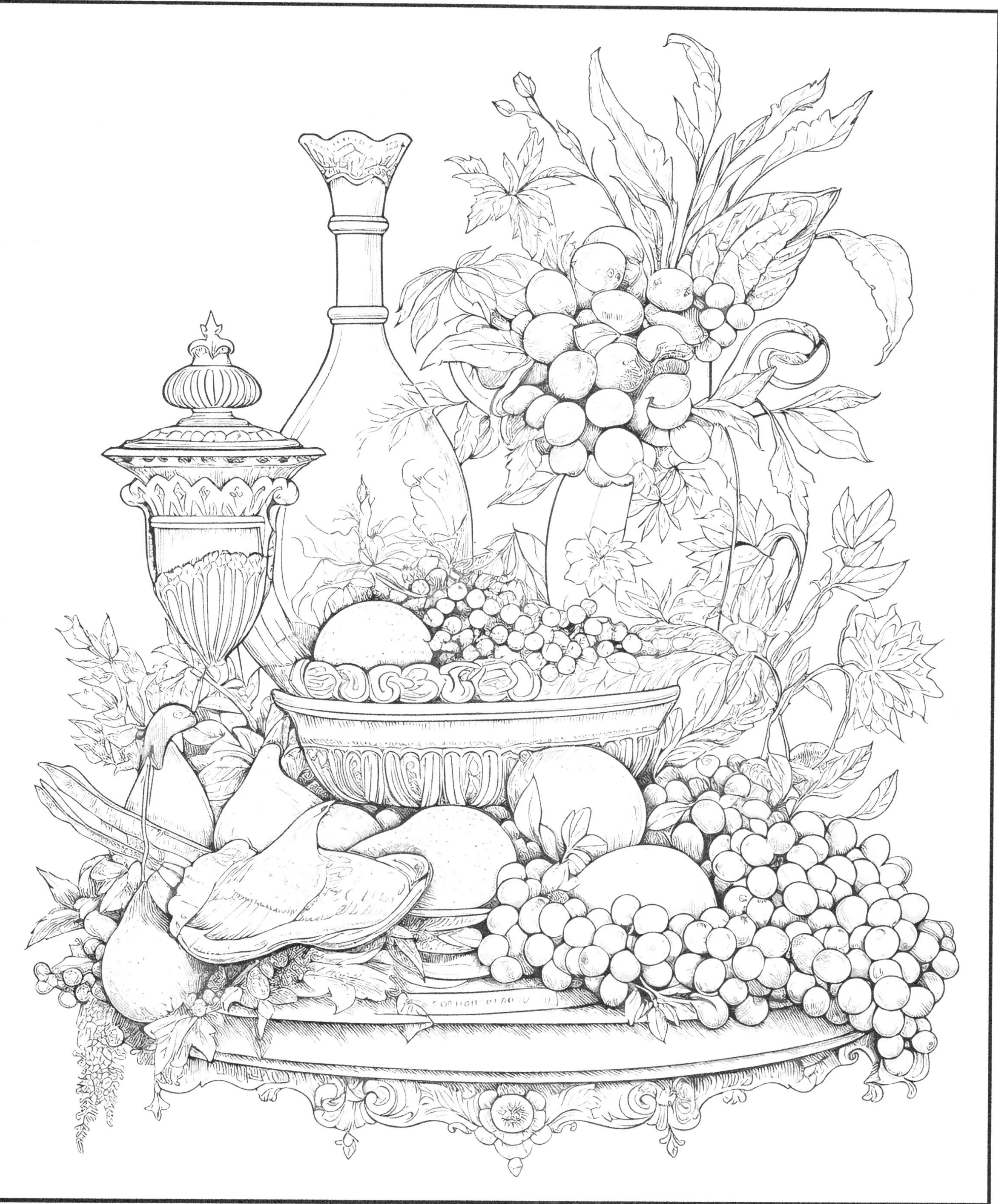

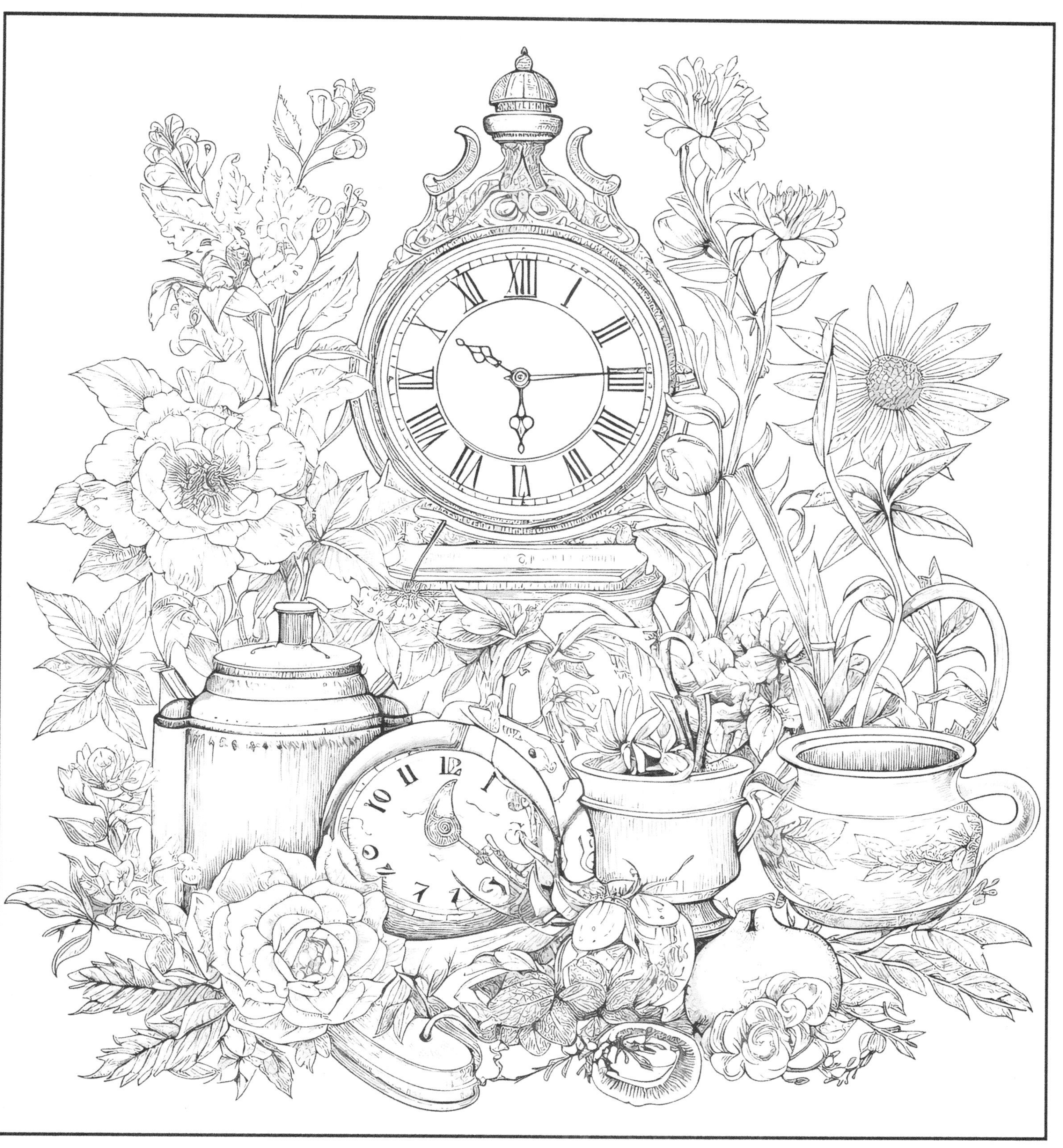

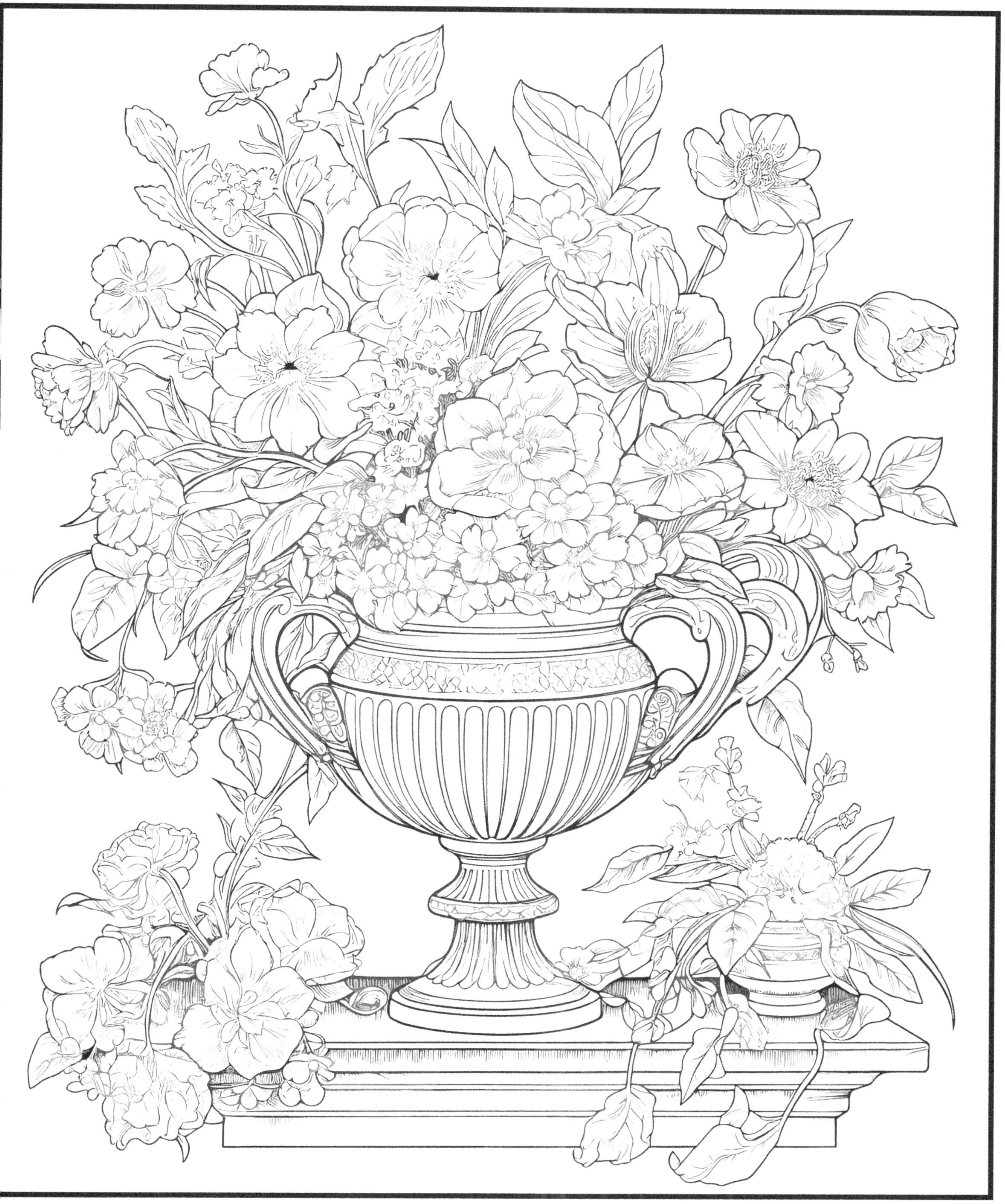

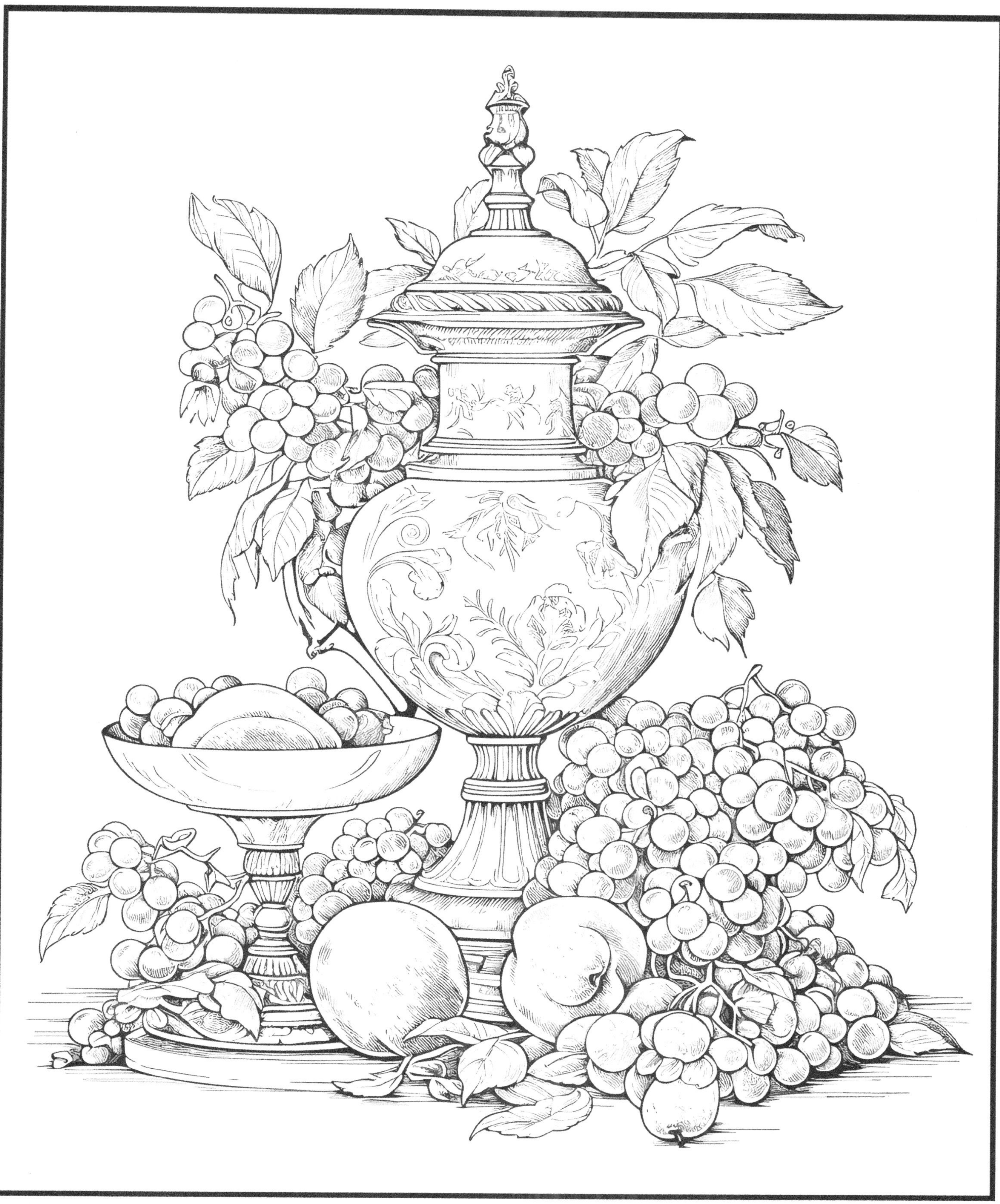

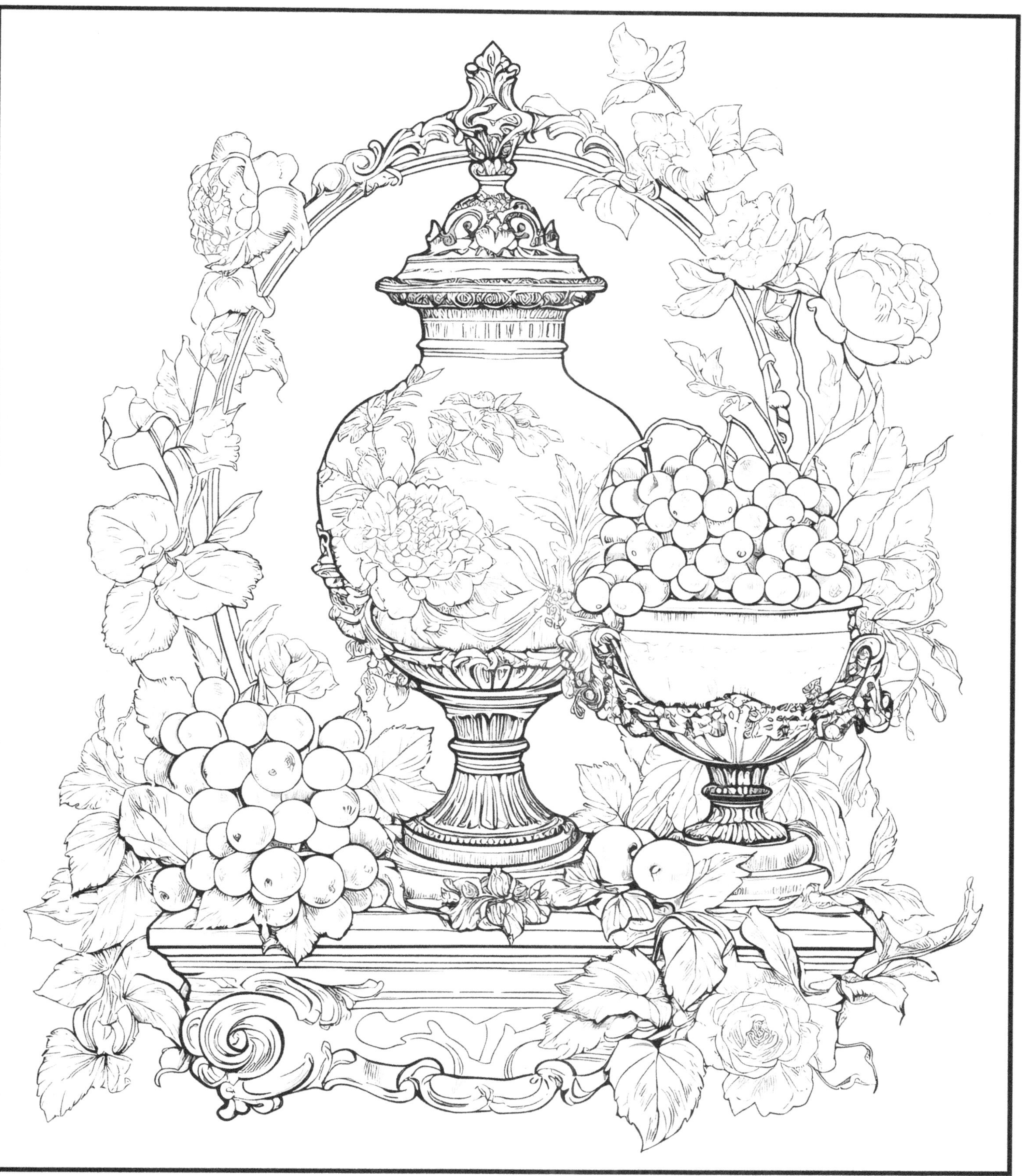

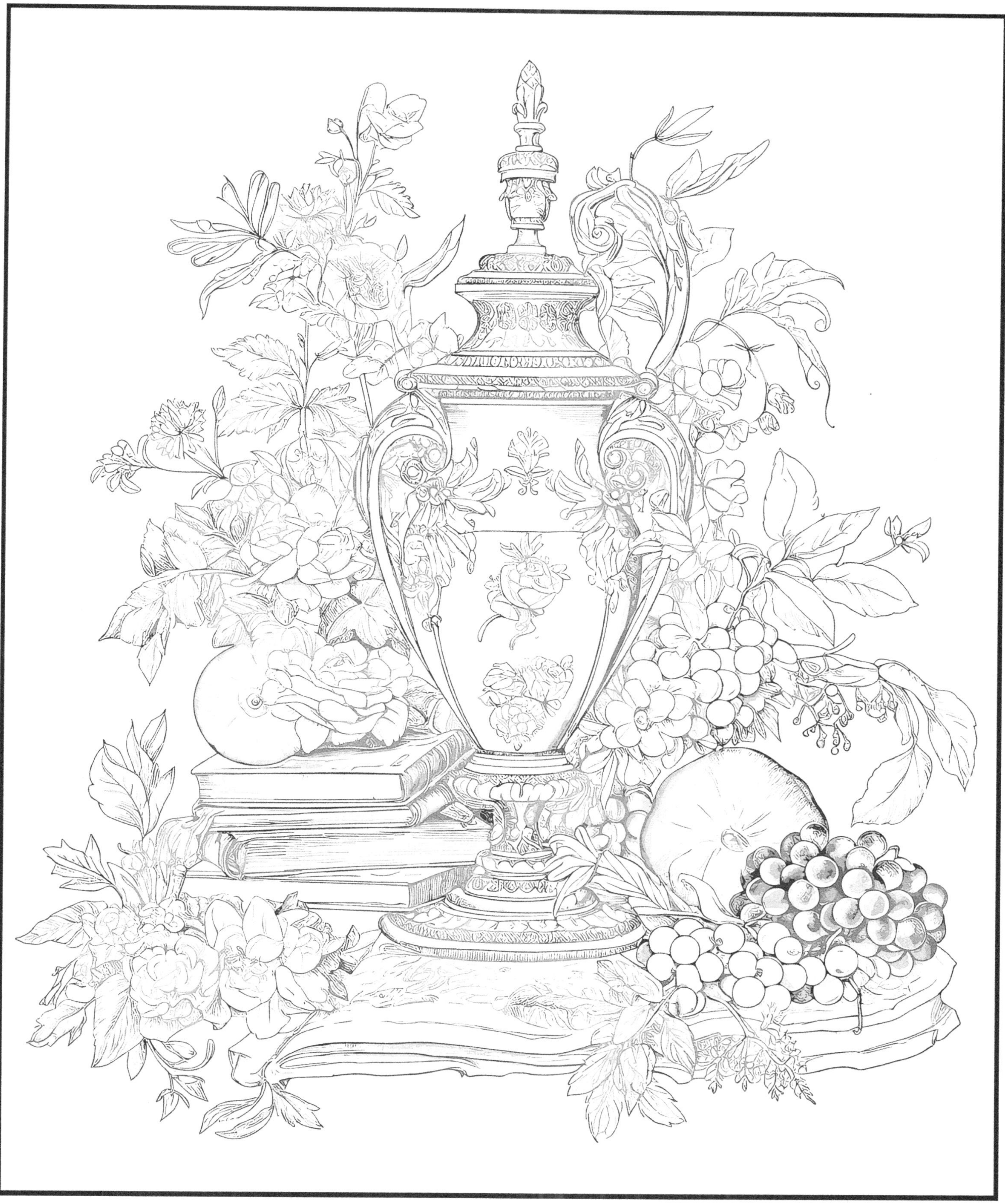

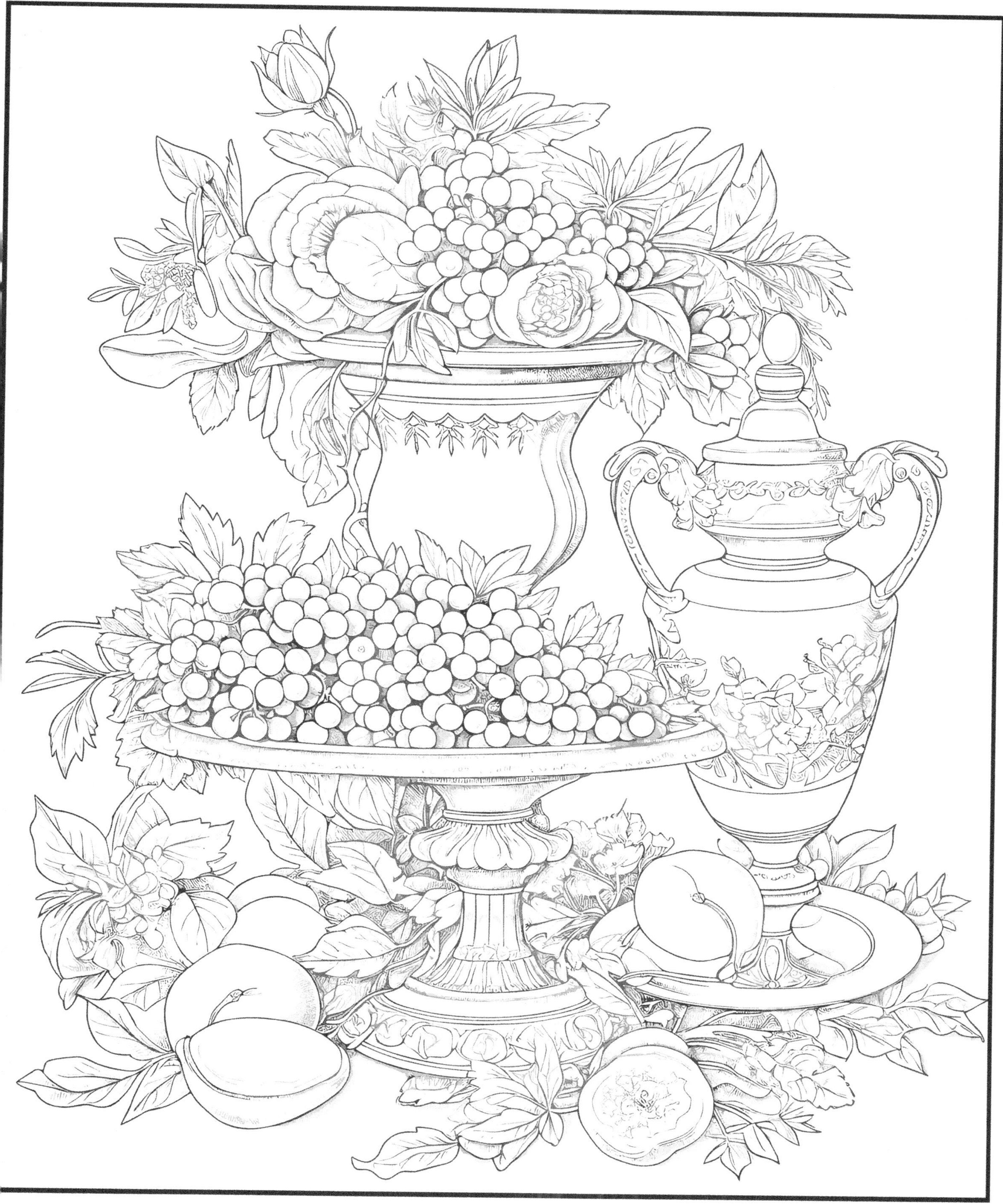

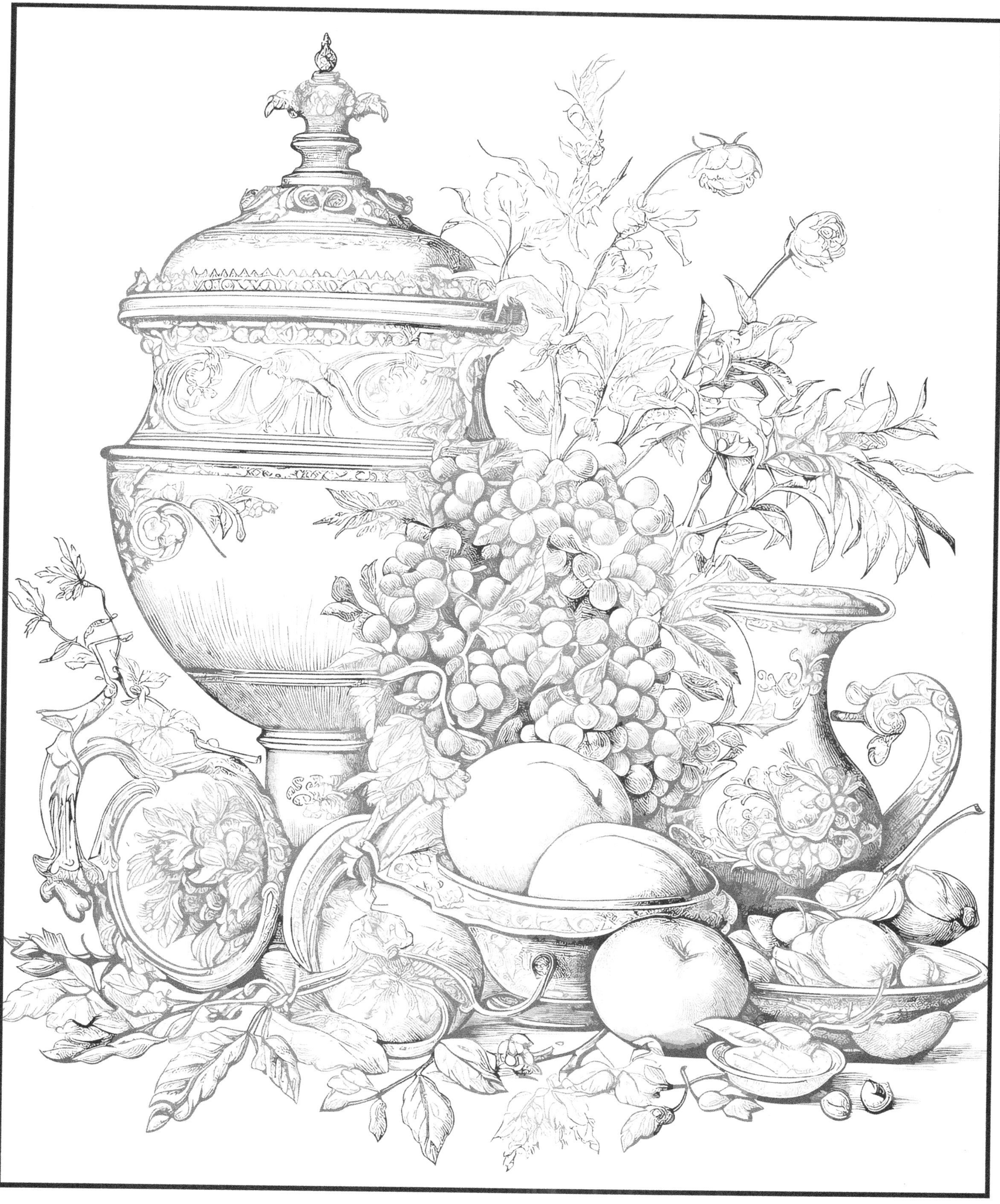

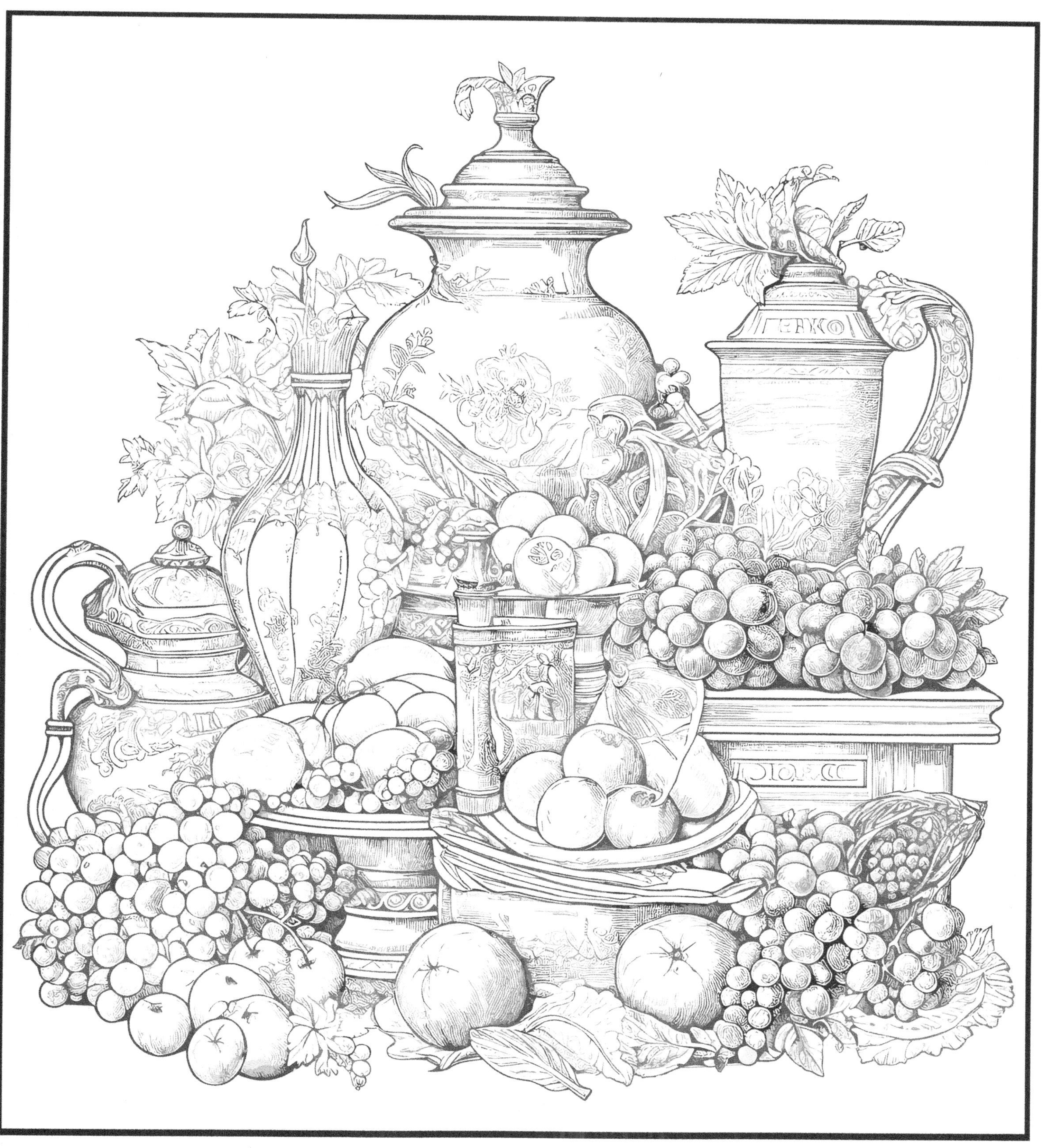

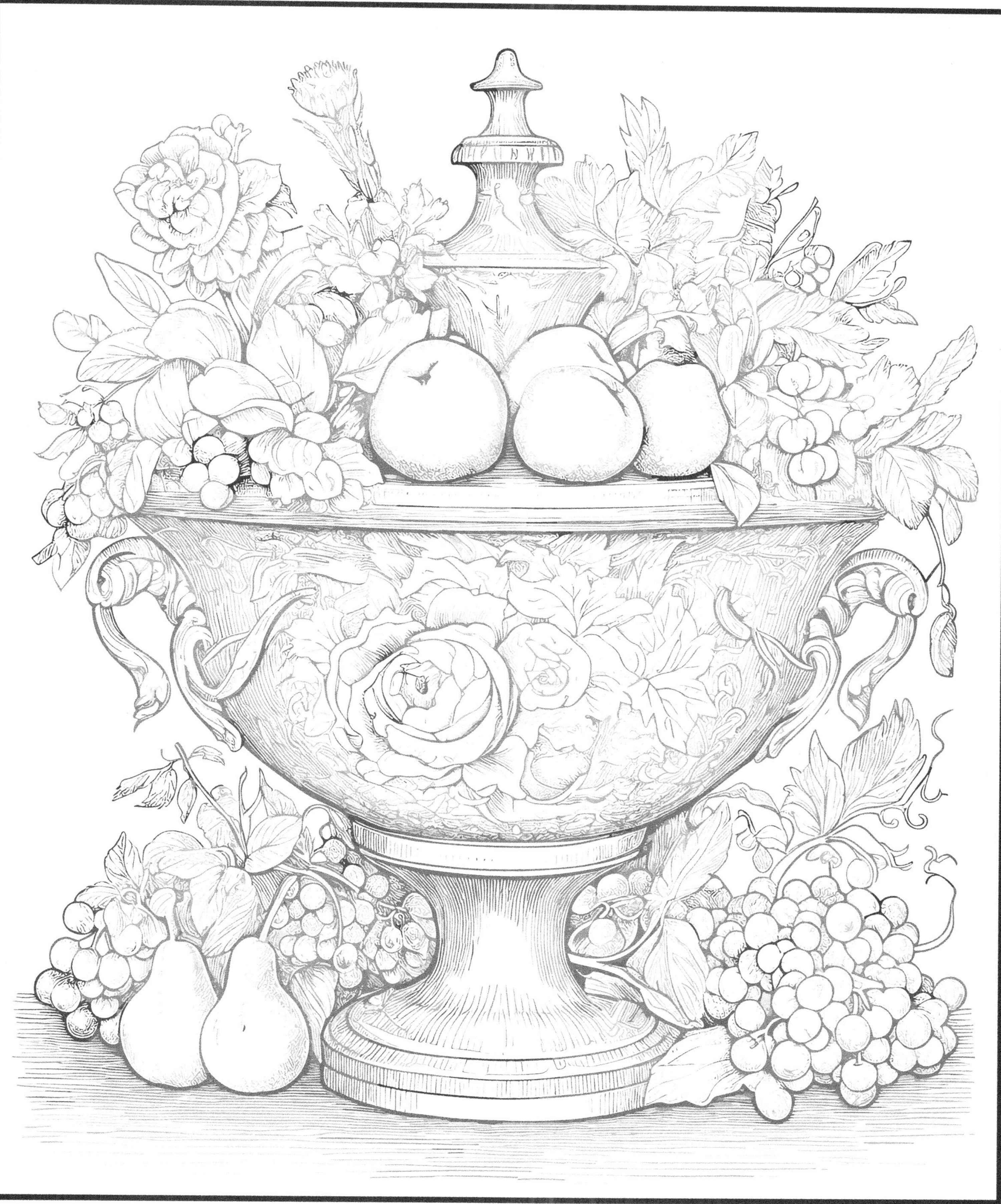

Made in the USA
Monee, IL
08 July 2026